A Deep but Dazzling Darkness

A Deep but Dazzling Darkness

An Anthology of Personal Experiences of God

EDITED BY

Lucy Lethbridge and Selina O'Grady

DARTON · LONGMAN + TODD

First published in 2002 by
Darton, Longman and Todd Ltd
1 Spencer Court
140–142 Wandsworth High Street
London sw18 4JJ

ISBN 0–232–52426–2

A catalogue record for this book is available from the British Library.

Set in 12/14.25pt Bembo
Designed and produced by Sandie Boccacci
using QuarkXPress on an Apple PowerMac

Printed and bound in Great Britain by
The Bath Press, Bath

Contents

Man is a dream about a shadow. But when some splendour falls upon him from God, a glory comes to him and his life is sweet.

Pindar, *c.*522–443 BC

Introduction

For two thousand years people searching for God have sought to find ways of describing their experiences of him. Sometimes, He is a still small voice, or a flooding light, or the unfathomable paradox that Henry Vaughan describes so vividly as 'a deep but dazzling darkness'. For the medieval mystics, Angela Foligno or Margery Kempe for example, the experience can be unnervingly real in its physical detail; for Wordsworth, Richard Jefferies or Ralph Waldo Emerson, it is in the experience of nature – the glorious sense of Creation surging through humanity. And each succeeding generation brings to its expression of that personal encounter with God, or the dreadful sense of God's absence, the flavour of its own time, distinct from those that have gone before. There is something uniquely seventeenth century about the morbid fears that God has deserted them described so graphically by Bunyan and the other Puritans. Only with the chipping of Lyle's geological hammer in the nineteenth century is this agony transmuted from the fear that God has deserted you to the dread that you must desert God. Which is not to say that no one ever experienced, for example, the dark night of the soul before St John of the Cross defined it, or thought of God as my 'sweeting' or 'my Beloved' before the thirteenth century ('my Beloved' is after all a term ripe with meaning from the Song of Solomon). Part of the joy of working on the book was hearing the echoes of previous ages as we worked chronologically through the centuries.

From the Old Testament to the present day the aim of this anthology has been to trace the personal relationship with God. And this relationship, for us, has meant not just the ecstasy of conversion, but the quieter consolation of belief affirmed, and the darker moments of doubt, despair and disbelief. Expressions of doubt in the existence of God are rare before the nineteenth century, the age of Mrs Humphrey Ward's novel of doubt *Robert Elsmere*, and its hero's sudden, terrible conviction that Christianity (which had up to then been his life) was 'a fairy tale'. But there are many agonising dark-night-of-the-soul experiences when God seems to be absent and darkness covers light, from the yearning of the Psalms, the permanent and haunting exile of the Anglo-Saxon Seafarer, to the torments of Gerard Manley Hopkins.

The challenge of compiling the anthology was to find extracts – poetry, letters, autobiography, fiction – which give voice to individual moments of this felt experience of God or God's absence and which also capture and reveal the flavour of each period. We have restricted ourselves to the Christian experience – or our anthology would have been limitless – but have tried to include as many branches of Christianity as we could.

Above all, we tried to find pieces that moved us – assuming that we could both agree on this (and after some disagreements we usually managed to) – but that also fitted the brief of the anthology as a whole. This of course meant that we have had to leave things out, and it has been a wrench to do so; many we have argued long about. Sometimes we have included extracts that were less vivid to us personally but were full of the flavour of the period. Sometimes we chose them because they were strikingly different, in one or two instances because they were funny. As with all anthologies, there are some notable omissions and there will also inevitably be lacunae of which we are unaware. We did not, for example, include George Herbert's peerlessly lovely poem 'Love' – not because it did not express the intimacy of an encounter with God because it does so wonderfully, but because it is, justly, among the most anthologised poems in English. Instead, we chose Herbert's lesser-known work 'The Search'. We hope that you will find this and many other pieces in the anthology as moving and revealing as we have.

LUCY LETHBRIDGE and SELINA O'GRADY
2002

From Genesis to Jeremiah

Genesis

And they heard the voice of the Lord God walking in the garden in the cool of the day: and Adam and his wife hid themselves from the presence of the Lord God amongst the trees of the garden.

And the Lord God called unto Adam, and said unto him, Where art thou?

And he said, I heard thy voice in the garden, and I was afraid, because I was naked; and I hid myself.

And he said, Who told thee that thou wast naked? Hast thou eaten of the tree, whereof I commanded thee that thou shouldest not eat?

And the man said, The woman whom thou gavest to be with me, she gave me of the tree, and I did eat.

And the Lord God said unto the woman, What is this that thou hast done? And the woman said, The serpent beguiled me, and I did eat.

And the Lord God said unto the serpent, Because thou hast done this, thou art cursed above all cattle, and above every beast of the field; upon thy belly shalt thou go, and dust shalt thou eat all the days of thy life:

And I will put enmity between thee and the woman, and

between thy seed and her seed; it shall bruise thy head, and thou shalt bruise his heel.

Unto the woman he said, I will greatly multiply thy sorrow and thy conception; in sorrow thou shalt bring forth children; and thy desire shall be to thy husband, and he shall rule over thee.

And unto Adam he said, Because thou hast hearkened unto the voice of thy wife, and hast eaten of the tree, of which I commanded thee, saying, Thou shalt not eat of it: cursed is the ground for thy sake; in sorrow shalt thou eat of it all the days of thy life;

Thorns also and thistles shall it bring forth to thee; and thou shalt eat the herb of the field;

In the sweat of thy face shalt thou eat bread, till thou return unto the ground; for out of it wast thou taken: for dust thou art, and unto dust shalt thou return.

3:8–19

And Jacob was left alone; and there wrestled a man with him until the breaking of the day.

And when he saw that he prevailed not against him, he touched the hollow of his thigh; and the hollow of Jacob's thigh was out of joint, as he wrestled with him.

And he said, Let me go, for the day breaketh. And he said, I will not let thee go, except thou bless me.

And he said unto him, What is thy name? And he said, Jacob.

And he said, Thy name shall be called no more Jacob, but Israel: for as a prince hast thou power with God and with men, and hast prevailed.

And Jacob asked him, and said, Tell me, I pray thee, thy name. And he said, Wherefore is it that thou dost ask after my name? And he blessed him there.

And Jacob called the name of the place Peniel: for I have seen God face to face, and my life is preserved.

32:24–30

Exodus

And Moses said unto God, Behold, when I come unto the children of Israel, and shall say unto them, The God of your fathers hath sent me unto you; and they shall say unto me, What is his name? What shall I say unto them?

And God said unto Moses, I AM THAT I AM: and he said, Thus shalt thou say unto the children of Israel, I AM hath sent me to you.

3:13–14

I Samuel

And the child Samuel ministered unto the Lord before Eli. And the word of the Lord was precious in those days; there was no open vision.

And it came to pass at that time, when Eli was laid down in his place, and his eyes began to wax dim, that he could not see;

And ere the lamp of God went out in the temple of the Lord, where the ark of God was, and Samuel was laid down to sleep;

That the Lord called Samuel: and he answered, Here am I.

And he ran unto Eli, and said, Here am I; for thou calledst me. And he said, I called not; lie down again. And he went and lay down.

And the Lord called yet again, Samuel. And Samuel arose and went to Eli, and said, Here am I; for thou didst call me. And he answered, I called not, my son; lie down again.

[3]

Now Samuel did not yet know the Lord, neither was the word of the Lord yet revealed unto him.

And the Lord called Samuel again the third time. And he arose and went to Eli, and said, Here am I; for thou didst call me. And Eli perceived that the Lord had called the child.

Therefore Eli said unto Samuel, Go, lie down: and it shall be, if he call thee, that thou shalt say, Speak, Lord; for thy servant heareth. So Samuel went and lay down in his place.

And the Lord came, and stood, and called as at other times, Samuel, Samuel. Then Samuel answered, Speak; for thy servant heareth.

3:1–10

I Kings

And he came thither unto a cave and lodged there; and behold, the word of the Lord came to him, and he said to him, What doest thou here Elijah?

And he said, I have been very jealous for the Lord God of hosts: for the children of Israel have forsaken thy covenant, thrown down thine altars, and slain thy prophets with the sword; and I, even I only, am left; and they seek my life to take it away.

And he said, Go forth and stand upon the mount before the Lord. And behold, the Lord passed by, and a great and strong wind rent the mountains and brake in pieces the rocks before the Lord; but the Lord was not in the wind: and after the wind an earthquake; but the Lord was not in the earthquake:

And after the earthquake a fire; but the Lord was not in the fire: and after the fire a still, small voice.

And it was so, when Elijah heard it that he wrapped his face in his mantle and went out and stood in the entering in

of the cave. And behold, there came a voice unto him, and
said, What doest thou here Elijah?

19:9–13

Job

Therefore I will not refrain my mouth; I will speak in the
anguish of my spirit; I will complain in the bitterness of my
soul.

Am I a sea, or a whale, that thou settest a watch over me?

When I say, My bed shall comfort me, my couch shall ease
my complaint;

Then thou scarest me with dreams, and terrifiest me
through visions:

So that my soul chooseth strangling, and death rather than
my life.

I loathe it; I would not live alway: let me alone; for my
days are vanity.

What is man, that thou shouldest magnify him? And that
thou shouldest set thine heart upon him?

And that thou shouldest visit him every morning and try
him every moment?

How long wilt thou not depart from me, nor let me alone
till I swallow down my spittle?

I have sinned; what shall I do unto thee, O thou preserver
of men? Why hast thou set me as a mark against thee, so that
I am a burden to myself?

And why dost thou not pardon my transgresssion, and
take away mine iniquity? For now shall I sleep in the dust;
and thou shalt seek me in the morning, but I shall not be.

7:11–21

Then the Lord answered Job out of the whirlwind and said,
Who is this that darkeneth counsel by words without knowledge?
Gird up now thy loins like a man; for I will demand of thee, and answer thou me.
Where wast thou when I laid the foundations of the earth? Declare, if thou hast understanding.
Who hath laid the measures thereof, if thou knowest? Or who hath stretched the line upon it?
Whereupon are the foundations thereof fastened? Or who laid the corner stone thereof;
When the morning stars sang together, and all the sons of God shouted for joy?

38:1–7

Then Job answered the Lord, and said,
I know that thou canst do every thing, and that no thought can be withholden from thee.
Who is he that hideth counsel without knowledge? Therefore have I uttered that I understood not; things too wonderful for me, which I knew not.
Hear, I beseech thee, and I will speak: I will demand of thee, and declare thou unto me.
I have heard of thee by the hearing of the ear: but now mine eye seeth thee.
Wherefore I abhor myself, and repent in dust and ashes.

42:1–6

Psalms

Deep calleth unto deep at the noise of thy waterspouts: all thy waves and thy billows are gone over me.
Yet the Lord will command his lovingkindness in the

daytime, and in the night his song shall be with me, and my
prayer unto the God of my life.

42:7–8

Save me, O God; for the waters are come in unto my soul.

I sink in deep mire, where there is no standing: I am come
into deep waters where the floods overflow me.

I am weary of my crying: my throat is dried: mine eyes fail
while I wait for my God.

69: 1–3

Out of the depths have I cried unto thee, O Lord.

Lord, hear my voice: let thine ears be attentive to the voice
of my supplications.

If thou, Lord, shouldest mark iniquities, O Lord, who shall
stand?

But there is forgiveness with thee, that thou mayest be
feared.

I wait for the Lord, my soul doth wait, and in his word do
I hope.

My soul waiteth for the Lord more than they that watch
for the morning;

I say, more than they that watch for the morning.

130:1–7

Lord, thou hast searched me and known me.

Thou knowest my downsitting and mine uprising, thou
understandest my thought afar off.

Thou compassest my path and my lying down, and art
acquainted with all my ways.

For there is not a word in my tongue, but lo, O Lord, thou
knowest it altogether.

[7]

Thou hast beset me behind and before, and laid thine hand upon me.

Such knowledge is too wonderful for me; it is high, I cannot attain to it.

Whither shall I go from thy spirit? Or whither shall I flee from thy presence?

If I ascend up into heaven, thou art there: if I make my bed in hell, behold thou art there.

If I take the winds of morning and dwell in the uttermost parts of the sea;

Even there shall thy hand lead me, and thy right hand shall hold me.

If I say, Surely the darkness shall cover me; even the night shall be light about me.

Yea, the darkness hideth not from thee; but the night shineth as the day: the darkness and the light are both alike to thee.

139:1–12

The Song of Solomon

The voice of my beloved! Behold, he cometh leaping upon the mountains, skipping upon the hills.

My beloved is like a roe or a young hart: behold, he standeth behind our wall, he looketh forth at the windows, shewing himself through the lattice.

My beloved spake, and said unto me, Rise up, my love, my fair one, and come away.

For lo, the winter is past, the rain is over and gone;

The flowers appear on the earth; the time of the singing of birds is come, and the voice of the turtle is heard in our land;

The fig tree putteth forth her green figs, and the vines with the tender grape give a good smell. Arise, my love, my fair one, and come away.

My dove, that art in the clefts of the rock, in the secret places of the stairs, let me see thy countenance, let me hear thy voice; for sweet is thy voice, and thy countenance is comely.

2:8–14

By night on my bed I sought him whom my soul loveth: I sought him, but I found him not.

I will rise now, and go about the city in the streets, and in the broad ways I will seek him whom my soul loveth: I sought him, but I found him not.

The watchmen that go about the city found me: to whom I said, Saw ye him whom my soul loveth?

It was but a little that I passed from them, but I found him whom my soul loveth: I held him, and would not let him go, until I had brought him into my mother's house, and into the chamber of her that conceived me.

3:1–4

Isaiah

In the year that King Uzziah died I saw also the Lord sitting upon a throne, high and lifted up and his train filled the temple.

Above it stood the seraphims; each one had six wings; with twain he covered his face, and with twain he covered his feet, and with twain he did fly.

And one cried unto another, and said, Holy, holy, holy, *is* the LORD of hosts: the whole earth *is* full of his glory.

And the posts of the door moved at the voice of him that cried; and the house was filled with smoke.

Then said I, Woe is me! For I am undone; because I am a man of unclean lips and I dwell in the midst of a people of unclean lips; for mine eyes have seen the King, the LORD of hosts.

Then flew one of the seraphims unto me, having a live coal in his hand, which he had taken with the tongs from off the altar:

And he laid it upon my mouth, and said, Lo, this hath touched thy lips; and thine iniquity is taken away and thy sin purged.

Also I heard the voice of the Lord, saying, Whom shall I send, and who will go for us? Then said I, Here am I: send me.

6:1–8

And the glory of the LORD shall be revealed, and all flesh shall see it together: for the mouth of the LORD hath spoken it.

The voice said, Cry. And he said, What shall I cry? All flesh is grass and all the goodliness thereof is as the flower of the field:

The grass withereth, the flower fadeth; because the spirit of the LORD bloweth upon it: surely the people is grass.

The grass withereth, the flower fadeth: but the word of our God shall stand for ever.

40:5–8

Jeremiah

Lord, thou hast deceived me, and I was deceived: thou art stronger than I, and hast prevailed: I am in derision daily, everyone mocketh me.

For since I spake, I cried out, I cried violence and spoil because the word of the Lord was made a reproach unto me and a derision, daily.

Then I said, I will not make mention of him, nor speak any more in his name. But his word was in my heart as a burning fire shut up in my bones, and I was weary with foreboding.

20:7–9

2

From St Matthew to
St Hesychios the Priest:
1st–7th century

Matthew

Then cometh Jesus with them unto a place called
Gethsemane, and saith unto the disciples, Sit ye here, while I
go and pray yonder.

And he took with him Peter and the two sons of Zebedee
and began to be sorrowful and very heavy.

Then saith he unto them, My soul is exceeding sorrowful, even unto death: tarry ye here, and watch with me.

And he went a little further, and fell on his face, and
prayed, saying, O my father, if it be possible, let this cup pass
from me: nevertheless not as I will, but as thou wilt.

And he cometh unto the disciples and findeth them
asleep, and saith unto Peter, What, could ye not watch with
me one hour?

Watch and pray, that ye enter not into temptation: the
spirit indeed is willing, but the flesh is weak.

He went away again the second time, and prayed, saying,
O my Father, if this cup may not pass from me, except I
drink it, thy will be done.

And he came and found them asleep again: for their eyes
were heavy.

And he left them, and went away again, and prayed the third time, saying the same words.

Then cometh he to his disciples, and saith unto them, Sleep on now and take your rest: behold, the hour is at hand, and the Son of man is betrayed into the hands of sinners.

Rise, let us be going: behold, he is at hand that doth betray me.

26:36–46

Mark

And it came to pass in those days, that Jesus came from Nazareth of Galilee, and was baptized of John in Jordan.

And straightway coming up out of the water, he saw the heavens opened, and the Spirit like a dove descending upon him:

And there came a voice from heaven, saying, Thou art my beloved Son in whom I am well pleased.

1:9–11

And when the sixth hour was come, there was darkness over the whole land until the ninth hour.

And at the ninth hour Jesus cried with a loud voice, saying, Eloi,. Eloi, lama sabachthani? Which is, being interpreted, My God, My God, why hast thou forsaken me?

And some of them that stood by, when they heard it, said, Behold, he calleth Elias.

And one ran and filled a sponge full of vinegar and put it on a reed, and gave him to drink, saying, Let alone; let us see whether Elias will come to take him down.

And Jesus cried with a loud voice and gave up the ghost.

15:34–37

Luke

And there were in the same country shepherds abiding in the field, keeping watch over their flock by night.

And lo, the angel of the Lord came upon them and the glory of the Lord shone round about them: and they were sore afraid.

And the angel said unto them, Fear not: for behold I bring you good tidings of great joy, which shall be to all people.

For unto you a child is born this day in the city of David a Saviour, which is Christ the Lord.

And this shall be a sign unto you: Ye shall find the babe wrapped in swaddling clothes, lying in a manger.

2:8–12

And behold, two of them went that same day to a village called Emmaus. Which was from Jerusalem about threescore furlongs.

And they talked together of all these things which had happened.

And it came to pass, that, while they communed together and reasoned, Jesus himself drew near, and went with them.

But their eyes were holden that they should not know him.

And he said unto them, What manner of communications are these that ye have one to another, as ye walk, and are sad?

And the one of them, whose name was Cleopas, answering said unto him, Art thou only a stranger in Jerusalem, and hast not known the things which are come to pass there in these days?

And he said unto them, What things? And they said unto him, Concerning Jesus of Nazareth which was a prophet mighty in deed and word before God and all the people:

And how the chief priests and our rulers delivered him to be condemned to death, and have crucified him.

But we trusted that it had been him which should have redeemed Israel; and beside all this, today is the third day since these things were done.

Yea, and certain women also of our company made us astonished, which were early at the sepulchre;

And when they found not his body, they came, saying that they had also seen a vision of angels, which said that he was alive.

And certain of them which were with us went to the sepulchre, and found it even so as the women had said: but him they saw not.

Then he said unto them, O fools, and slow of heart to believe all that the prophets have spoken:

Ought not Christ to have suffered these things, and to enter into his glory?

And beginning at Moses and all the prophets, he expounded unto them in all the scriptures the things concerning himself.

And they drew nigh unto the village, whither they went: and he made as though he would have gone further.

But they constrained him, saying, Abide with us: for it is toward evening, and the day is far spent. And he went in to tarry with them.

And it came to pass, as he sat at meat with them, he took the bread and blessed it, and brake and gave to them.

And their eyes were opened, and they knew him; and he vanished out of their sight.

24:13–31

John

The next day John seeth Jesus coming unto him, and saith, Behold the Lamb of God, which taketh away the sin of the world.

This is he of whom I said, after me cometh a man which is preferred before me: for he was before me.

And I knew him not; but that he should be made manifest to Israel, therefore am I come baptizing with water.

And John bare record, saying, I saw the Spirit descending from heaven like a dove, and it abode upon him.

And I knew him not: but he that sent me to baptize with water, the same said unto me, Upon whom thou shalt see the Spirit descending, and remaining on him, the same is he which baptizeth with the Holy Ghost.

And I saw, and bare record that this is the Son of God.

Again the next day after John stood and two of his disciples;

And looking upon Jesus as he walked, he saith, Behold the Lamb of God.

1:29–36

There cometh a woman of Samaria to draw water; Jesus saith unto her, Give me to drink.

(For his disciples were gone away unto the city to buy meat.)

Then saith the woman of Samaria unto him, How is it that thou, being a Jew, askest drink of me, which am a woman of Samaria? For the Jews have no dealings with the Samaritans.

Jesus answered and said unto her, If thou knewest the gift of God, and who it is that saith to thee, Give me to drink; thou wouldest have asked of him, and he would have given thee living water.

The woman saith unto him, Sir, thou hast nothing to draw with, and the well is deep; from whence then hast thou that living water?

Art thou greater than our father Jacob which gave us the well, and drank thereof himself, and his children and his cattle?

Jesus answered and said unto her, Whosoever drinketh of this water shall thirst again:

But whosoever drinketh of the water that I shall give him shall never thirst; but the water that I shall give him shall be in him a well of water springing up into everlasting life.

The woman saith unto him, Sir, give me this water, that I thirst not, neither come hither to draw.

Jesus saith unto her, Go, call thy husband and come hither.

The woman answered and said, I have no husband. Jesus said unto her, Thou hast well said, I have no husband:

For thou hast had five husbands; and he whom thou now hast is not thy husband: in that saidst thou truly.

The woman saith unto him, Sir, I perceive that thou art a prophet.

Our fathers worshipped in this mountain; and ye say that in Jerusalem is the place where men ought to worship.

Jesus saith unto her, Woman, believe me, the hour cometh, when ye shall neither in this mountain nor yet at Jerusalem, worship the Father.

Ye worship ye know not what: we know what we worship: for salvation is of the Jews.

But the hour cometh, and now is, when the true worshippers shall worship the Father in spirit and in truth: for the Father seeketh such to worship him.

God is a spirit: and they that worship him must worship him in spirit and in truth.

The woman saith unto him, I know that Messias cometh, which is called Christ: when he is come, he will tell us all things.

Jesus saith unto her, I that speak unto thee am he.

And upon this came his disciples and marvelled that he talked with the woman: yet no man said, What seekest her thou? Or, Why talkest thou with her?

The woman then left her waterpot and went her way into the city and saith to the men,

Come, see a man, which told me all things that ever I did: is not this the Christ?

4:7–29

But Mary stood without at the sepulchre weeping: and as she wept, she stooped down, and looked into the sepulchre.

And seeth two angels in white sitting, the one at the head, and the other at the feet, where the body of Jesus had lain.

And they say unto her, Woman, why weepest thou? She saith unto them, Because they have taken away my Lord and I know not where they have laid him.

And when she had thus said, she turned herself back and saw Jesus standing and knew not that it was Jesus.

Jesus saith unto her, Woman, why weepest thou? Whom seekest thou? She, supposing him to be the gardener, saith unto him, Sir, if thou have borne him hence, tell me where thou hast laid him, and I will take him away.

Jesus saith unto her, Mary. She turned herself, and saith unto him, Rabboni; which is to say, Master.

20:11–16

But Thomas, one of the twelve, called Didymus, was not with them when Jesus came.

The other disciples therefore said unto him, We have seen the Lord. But he said unto them, Except I shall see in his hands the print of the nails, and put my finger into the print of the nails and thrust my hand into his side, I will not believe.

And after eight days again his disciples were within, and Thomas was with them: then came Jesus, the doors being shut and stood in the midst and said, Peace be unto you.

Then saith he to Thomas, Reach hither thy finger and behold my hands; and reach hither thy hand and thrust it into my side: and be not faithless but believing.

And Thomas answered and said unto him, My Lord and my God.

20:24–28

Acts

And when the day of Pentecost was fully come, they were all with one accord in one place.

And suddenly there came a sound from heaven as of a rushing mighty wind, and it filled all the house where they were sitting.

And there appeared unto them cloven tongues like as of fire, and it sat upon each of them.

And they were all filled with the Holy Ghost, and began to speak with other tongues, as the Spirit gave them utterance.

2:1–4

And Saul, yet breathing out threatenings and slaughter against the disciples of the Lord, went unto the high priest.

And desired of him letters to Damascus to the synagogues, that if he found any of this way, whether they were men or women, he might bring them bound unto Jerusalem.

And as he journeyed, he came near Damascus; and suddenly there shined round about him a light from heaven:

And he fell to the earth, and heard a voice saying unto him, Saul, Saul, why persecutest thou me?

And he said, Who art thou, Lord? And the Lord said, I am Jesus whom thou persecutest: it is hard for thee to kick against the pricks.

And he trembling and astonished said, Lord, what wilt thou have me to do? And the Lord said unto him, Arise and go into the city, and it shall be told thee what thou must do.

And the men which journeyed with him stood speechless, hearing a voice but seeing no man.

And Saul arose from the earth; and when his eyes were opened, he saw no man: but they led him by the hand, and brought him into Damascus.

9:1–18

I Corinthians

For now we see through a glass darkly; but then face to face: now I know in part; but then shall I know even as also I am known.

13:12

II Corinthians

Therefore if any man be in Christ, he is a new creature: old things are passed away; behold, all things are become new.

5:17

Galatians

I am crucified with Christ: nevertheless I live; yet not I, but Christ liveth in me: and the life which I now live in the flesh

I live by the faith of the Son of God, who loved me, and gave himself for me.

I do not frustrate the grace of God: for if righteousness come by the law, then Christ is dead in vain.

2:20

I John

Beloved, let us love one another: for love is of God; and every one that loveth is born of God, and knoweth God.

He that loveth not knoweth not God; for God is love.

4:7–8

The Apocryphal New Testament

The letter of Pilate to Herod

It was no good thing which I did at your persuasion when I crucified Jesus. I ascertained from the centurion and the soldiers that he rose again, and I sent to Galilee and learned that he was preaching there to above five hundred believers.

My wife Procla took Longinus, the believing centurion, and ten (or twelve) soldiers (who had kept the sepulchre), and went forth and found him 'sitting in a tilled field' teaching a multitude. He saw them, addressed them, and spoke of his victory over death and hell. Procla and the rest returned and told me. I was in great distress, and put on a mourning garment and went with her and fifty soldiers to Galilee. We found Jesus: and as we approached him there was a sound in heaven and thunder, and the earth trembled and gave forth a sweet odour. We fell on our faces and the Lord came and raised us up, and I saw on him the scars of the passion, and he laid his hands on my shoulders, saying: All generations and families shall call thee blessed, because in thy days the Son of Man died and rose again.

Other Appendixes to the Acts of Pilate

They did many evil things to Jesus that night, and on the dawn of Friday delivered him to Pilate. He was condemned and crucified with the two robbers, Gestas on the left, Demas on the right.

He on the left cried out to Jesus: See what evils I have wrought on the earth; and had I known thou wert the king, I would have killed thee too. Why callest thou thyself Son of God and canst not help thyself in the hour of need or how canst thou succour any other that prayeth? If thou be the Christ, come down from the cross that I may believe thee . . .

But Demas on the right, seeing the divine grace of Jesus, began to cry out thus: I know thee, Jesus Christ, that thou art the Son of God. I see thee, Christ, worshipped by ten thousand times ten thousand angels; forgive my sins that I have committed: make not the stars to enter into judgement with me, or moon, when thou judgest all the world . . .

And when the thief had so said, Jesus saith unto him: Verily, verily, I say unto thee, Demas, that to-day thou shalt be with me in paradise.

Other Appendixes to the Acts of Pilate

The Gospel of Eve

I stood upon a high mountain and saw a tall man, and another of short stature, and heard something like the sound of thunder and went nearer in order to hear. Then he spoke to me and said: I am thou and thou art I, and wherever thou art, there am I, and I am sown in all things; and whence thou wilt, thou gatherest me, but when thou gatherest me, then gatherest thou thyself.

St Ignatius of Antioch
c.35–c.107

Letter to the Romans Before his Martyrdom in the Colosseum

I am writing to all the Churches to tell them that I am, with all my heart, to die for God – if only you do not prevent it. I beseech you not to indulge your benevolence at the wrong time. Please let me be thrown to the wild beasts; through them I can reach God. I am God's wheat; I am ground by the teeth of the wild beasts that I may end as the pure bread of Christ. If anything, coax the beasts on to become my sepulchre and to leave nothing of my body undevoured so that, when I am dead, I may be no bother to anyone. I shall be really a disciple of Jesus Christ if and when the world can no longer see so much as my body. Make petition then, to the Lord for me, so that by these means I may be made a sacrifice to God. I do not command you as Peter and Paul did. They were Apostles; I am a condemned man. They were free men; I am still a slave. Still, if I suffer, I shall be emancipated by Jesus Christ and, in my resurrection, shall be free. But now in chains I am learning to have no wishes of my own.

A stream flows
Whispering inside me;
Deep within me it says:
Come to the Father.

St Mary of Egypt
3rd century

... he [the priest Zossima] saw that there really was some kind of being walking along at midday. It was a woman [Mary of Egypt] and she was naked, her body black as if scorched by the fierce heat of the sun, the hair on her head was white as wool and short, coming only down to the neck.

... Then the woman began to tell him what had happened to her, thus:

'My homeland, father, was Egypt. I lived with my parents but when I was only twelve years old I spurned their care and went into Alexandria. I am ashamed to think how I lost my virginity there and how I was on fire with untiring and clamorous desire for lust ... For more than seventeen years, I spent my life openly tarrying in the fires of lust ...

'Now when the festival of the Exaltation of the Precious Cross [in Jerusalem] came round and I was going about as usual hunting for the souls of young men, I saw at first light that everyone was going to the church. So I went along, running with those who were running there and I came with them into the forecourt of the Cathedral. At the hour for the Exaltation of the Holy Cross I pushed and was pushed, fighting my way fiercely through the crowd to get in. So somehow, I, unhappy wretch that I was, came near to where the life-giving wood was being displayed.

'... All the rest went in [to the cathedral] without difficulty, with no impediment, but as soon as I set foot on the threshold of the church, it refused to admit me. It was as if a detachment of soldiers stood in the way to prevent me from entering; some unexplained power repelled me and I stood again in the forecourt. I suffered this again three or four times and at last, worn out, I gave up pushing and being pushed back ... I drew back and stood in a corner of the forecourt. And only then did I begin to see why I was being prevented from going in to see the life-giving wood. For a salutary understanding touched my mind and the eyes of my heart and shewed me that it was the sinfulness of my actions that prevented me from going in. So I began to weep and grieve and beat my breast; I drew sighs and tears from the bottom of my heart. And then I saw in the place where I was standing, a picture of the holy Mother of God. Gazing directly into her eyes, I said, "Virgin and Lady, who gave birth to the Word of God according to the flesh, I see now that it is not suitable or decent for me, defiled as I am, to look upon this picture of you, ever immaculate Virgin ... But God, to whom you gave birth became man, as I have heard, to save sinners and to call them to repentance; so help me, for I am alone and without any other help. Receive my confession, and give me leave to enter the church and do not deprive me of the sight of that most precious wood upon which was fixed God made man, whom you carried and bore as a Virgin and where He gave His blood for my redemption. O Lady, let the doors be opened so that I might adore the divine cross."

'. . . At that point a great terror and stupor came over me, and I trembled all over, but when I came to the door which until then had been closed to me, it was as if all the force that had previously prevented me from entering now allowed me to go in. So I was admitted without hindrance and went in to the holy of holies and I was found worthy to worship the mystery of the precious and life-giving Wood of the Cross.'

. . . Zossima asked her, 'How many years have passed, my Lady, since you began to live in the desert?' The woman replied, 'I think it is forty seven years since I left the holy city.' Zossima asked her, 'And what have you been able to find to eat, my lady?' The woman replied, 'I was carrying two and a half loaves when I crossed the Jordan and after a while

they became hard as stones and I have gone on eating a little
of them at a time for all these years.'

Life of St Mary of Egypt

Paul the Simple
d. 339

One day he went to a monastery to visit it and to make himself useful to the brethren. After the customary conference,
the brothers entered the holy church of God to perform the
synaxis [the liturgical office said by monks] there, as usual.
Blessed Paul looked carefully at each of those who entered
the church, observing the spiritual disposition with which
they went to the *synaxis*, for he had received the grace from
the Lord of seeing the state of each one's soul, just as we see
their faces. When all had entered with sparkling eyes and
shining faces, with each one's angel rejoicing over him, he
said, 'I see one who is black and his whole body is dark; the
demons are standing on each side of him, dominating him,
drawing him to them, and leading him by the nose, and his
angel, filled with grief, with head bowed, follows him at a
distance.' Then Paul in tears beat his breast and sat down in
front of the church, weeping bitterly over him whom he had
seen ... Shortly after the end of the *synaxis*, as everyone was
coming out, Paul scrutinized each one, wanting to know in
what state they were coming away. He saw that man,
previously black and gloomy, coming out of the church with
a shining face and white body, the demons accompanying
him only at a distance, while his holy angel was following
close to him, rejoicing greatly over him. Then Paul leaped for
joy and began to cry out, blessing God, 'O the ineffable
loving-kindness and goodness of God!'

The Sayings of the Desert Fathers:
The Alphabetical Collection

St Augustine
354–430

Truth, truth: how in my inmost being the very marrow of my mind sighed for you!

Confessions III

I was caught up to Thee by Thy Beauty, and dragged back by my own weight; and fell once more with a groan to the world of sense.

Confessions VII

I was twisting and turning in my chain until it would break completely: I was now only a little bit held by it, but I was still held. You, Lord, put pressure on me in my hidden depths with a severe mercy wielding the double whip of fear and shame, lest I should again succumb, and lest that tiny and tenuous bond which still remained should not be broken, but once more regain strength and bind me even more firmly. Inwardly I said to myself: Let it be now, let it be now. And by this phrase I was already moving towards a decision; I had almost taken it, and then I did not do so. Yet I did not relapse into my original condition, but stood my ground very close to the point of deciding and recovered my breath. Once more I made the attempt and came only a little short of my goal; only a little short of it – yet I did not touch it or hold on to it. I was hesitating whether to die to death and to live to life. Ingrained evil had more hold over me than unaccustomed good. The nearer approached the moment of time when I would become different, the greater the horror of it struck me. But it did not thrust me back nor turn me away, but left me in a state of suspense.

Confessions VIII

What then do I love, when I love Thee? ... I love a certain light, and a certain voice, a certain fragrance, a certain food, a certain embrace when I love my God: a light, voice, fragrance, food, embrace of the inner man. Where that shines upon my soul which space cannot contain, that sounds which time cannot sweep away, that is fragrant which is scattered not by the breeze, that tastes sweet which when fed upon is not diminished, that clings close which no satiety disparts. This it is that I love, when I love my God!

Confessions X

Late have I loved you, beauty so old and so new: late have I loved you. And see, you were within and I was in the external world and sought you there, and in my unlovely state I plunged into those lovely created things which you made. You were with me, and I was not with you. The lovely things kept me far from you, though if they did not have their existence in you, they had no existence at all. You called and cried out loud and shattered my deafness. You were radiant and resplendent, you put to flight my blindness. You were fragrant, and I drew in my breath and now pant after you. I tasted you, and I feel but hunger and thirst for you. You touched me, and I am set on fire to attain the peace which is yours.

Confessions X

St Makarios of Egypt
4th century

There is a certain cloud-like power, fine as air, that lightly covers the intellect; and even though the lamp of grace always burns and shines in a man, as we said, yet this power covers its light like a veil in such a way that he is forced to confess that he is not perfect or wholly free from sin, but is, so to speak, both free and not free. This, certainly, does not happen without God's assent but is, on the contrary, in accordance with divine providence. Sometimes the dividing wall (cf. Eph. 2:14) is loosened and shattered, sometimes it is not entirely broken down. Nor is prayer always equally effective: sometimes grace is kindled more brightly, confers greater blessings, and refreshes more fully, and sometimes it is duller and less strong, as grace itself ordains according to what is of most profit to the person concerned. At certain times I have attained the level of perfection and have tasted and experienced the age to be; but never yet have I known any Christian who is perfect or absolutely free.

The Philokalia

John Cassian

c.360–c.435

Sometimes the mind hides itself in complete silence within the secrets of a profound quiet, so that the amazement of a sudden illumination chokes all sound of words and the over-awed spirit either keeps all its feelings to itself, or loses them and pours forth its desires to God with groanings that cannot be uttered.

Conferences

Abba Silvanus

d. c.414

The disciple of Abba Silvanus, Sachary, went in and found him in ecstasy with his hands stretched up to heaven. Closing the door he went out. He came back at the sixth and the ninth hour and found him in the same state. At the tenth hour he knocked, went in and found him inwardly at peace. So he said to him, 'How have you been today, Father?' Silvanus replied, 'I was carried up to heaven and saw the glory of God. And I stayed there until just now. And now I am dissolved.'

Lives of the Fathers

St Anatolius of Constantinople
d. 458

Fierce was the wild billow, dark was the night,
Oars laboured heavily, foam glimmered white;
Mariners trembled, peril was nigh:
Then said the God of Gods, 'Peace, it is I!'
...
Jesu, Deliverer! Come Thou to me;
Soothe Thou my voyaging over life's sea:
Thou, when the storm of death roars sweeping by,
Whisper, O Truth of Truth, 'Peace, it is I!'

St Maximos the Confessor
580–662

As long as I remain imperfect and refractory, neither obeying God by practising the commandments nor becoming perfect in spiritual knowledge, Christ from my point of view also appears imperfect and refractory because of me. For I diminish and cripple Him by not growing in spirit with Him, since I am 'the body of Christ and one of its members' (1 Cor. 12:27).

The Philokalia

Isaac of Nineveh or Isaac of Syria
7th century

What comes after them [the tongue and the petitions of the heart in prayer] is the entering into the treasury. Here, then, all mouths and tongues are silent, and the heart, the treasurer of the thoughts, the mind, the governor of the senses, the daring spirit, that swift bird, and all their means and powers ... have to stand still there; for the Master of the house has come.

Mystical Treatises

Many are avidly seeking but they alone find who remain in continual silence. Every man who delights in a multitude of words, even though he says admirable things, is empty within. If you love truth be a lover of silence. Silence like the sunlight will illuminate you in God and deliver you from the phantom of ignorance. Silence will unite you with God himself. More than all things love silence, it brings you a fruit that tongue cannot describe. In the beginning we have to force ourselves to be silent and then there is born something which draws us to silence. May God give you an experience of this some-thing which is born of silence. If only you will practise this, untold light will dawn on you as a consequence. After a while a certain sweetness is born in the heart of this exercise and the body is drawn almost by force to remain in silence.

St John of Karpathos
7th(?) century

It may happen that for a certain time a man is illumined and refreshed by God's grace, and then this grace is withdrawn. This makes him inwardly confused and he starts to grumble;

instead of seeking through steadfast prayer to recover his assurance of salvation, he loses patience and gives up. He is like a beggar who receives alms from the palace, and feels put out because he was not asked inside to dine with the king. 'Blessed are those who have not seen, and yet have believed' (John 20:29). Blessed also are those who, when grace is withdrawn, find no consolation in themselves, but only continuing tribulation and thick darkness, and yet do not despair; but, strengthened by faith, they endure courageously, convinced that they do indeed see Him who is invisible.

The Philokalia

St Hesychios the Priest
8th or 9th century

While we are strengthened in Christ Jesus and beginning to move forward in steadfast watchfulness, He at first appears in our intellect like a torch which, carried in the hand of the intellect, guides us along the tracks of the mind; then He appears like a full moon, circling the heart's firmament; then He appears to us like the sun, radiating justice, clearly revealing Himself in the full light of spiritual vision.

The Philokalia

3

From Bede to
St Symeon:
7th–11th century

Bede
673–735

The bishop being alone, reading or praying in the oratory of
that place, on a sudden, as he afterwards would say, he heard
the voice of persons singing most sweetly and rejoicing and
appearing to descend from heaven to earth. This voice he
said he first heard coming from the southeast, that is from
the point where the winter sun rises, and that afterwards it
drew near him till it came to the roof of the oratory where
the bishop was, and, entering therein, filled the same and all
about it. He listened attentively to what he heard, and after
about half an hour perceived the same song of joy ascend
from the roof of the said oratory, and return to heaven, with
inexpressible sweetness, the same way it came.

Life and Death of St Chad

The Story of Caedmon the Herdsman and Poet

In the monastery of this abbess there was a certain brother
specially distinguished by the divine grace, in that he used to
compose songs suited to religion and piety ... By his songs

the minds of many were often fired with contempt of the world and with desire for the heavenly life ... he did not learn that art of singing from men, nor taught by man, but he received freely by divine aid the gift of singing ... he had lived in the secular habit until he was well advanced in years, and had never learnt anything of versifying; and for this reason sometimes at an entertainment, when it was resolved for the sake of merriment that all should sing in turn, if he saw the harp approaching him, he would rise from the feast and go out and return home.

When he did this on one occasion, and having left the house where the entertainment was, had gone to the stable of the cattle which had been committed to his charge that night, and there at the proper time had composed himself to rest, there appeared to him someone in his sleep, and greeting him and calling him by his name, he said 'Caedmon, sing me something.' But he replied: 'I cannot sing; and for this reason I left the entertainment and came away here, because I could not sing.' Then he who was speaking to him replied: 'Nevertheless, you must sing to me.' 'What', he said, 'must I sing?' And the other said: 'Sing me of the beginning of creation.' On receiving this answer, he at once began to sing in praise of God the Creator, verses which he had never heard, of which this is the sense Awakening from his sleep, he remembered all that he had sung when sleeping and soon added more words in the same manner in song worthy of God ... And remembering all that he could learn by listening, and like, as it were, a clean animal chewing the cud, he turned it into the most harmonious song, and sweetly singing it, he made his teachers in their turn, his hearers.

Historia Ecclesiastica Gentis Anglorum

Letter from Pope Boniface to King Edwin of Northumbria

To the illustrious Edwin, King of the English: Boniface, Bishop, servant of the servants of God.

The words of man can never express the power of the supreme Divinity, abiding in His own greatness, invisible, inscrutable, eternal, such that no human intelligence can understand or define how great it is. Nevertheless, God's humanity having opened the doors of man's heart to admit Him, mercifully infuses into their minds by secret inspiration some knowledge of Himself. Accordingly, we have undertaken to extend our priestly responsibility to disclose to you the fullness of the Christian Faith, in order that we may impart to your senses also the Gospel of Christ, which our Saviour commanded to be preached to all nations, and may offer you the medicine of salvation.

Historia Ecclesiastica Gentis Anglorum

from **The Seafarer**
8th century

The prosperous man knows not
What some men endure who tread
The paths of exile to the end of the world.

Wherefore my heart leaps within me,
My mind roams with the waves
Over the whale's domain, it wanders far and wide
Across the face of the earth, returns again to me
Eager and unsatisfied; the solitary bird screams,
Irresistible, urges the heart to the whale's way
Over the stretch of the seas.

So it is that the joys
Of the Lord inspire me more than this dead life,
Ephemeral on earth.

Anon

from St Patrick's Breastplate
8th century

Christ guard me today
from poison, from burning,
from drowning, from hurt,
that I have my reward,

Christ beside me,
  Christ before me,
    Christ behind me,

Christ within me,
  Christ beneath me,
    Christ above me,

Christ on my right hand,
  Christ on my left,

Christ where I lie,
  Christ where I sit,
    Christ where I rise,

Christ in the hearts of all who think of me,
Christ in the mouths of all who speak to me,
Christ in every eye that sees me,
Christ in every ear that hears me.

Today I put on
a terrible strength,
invoking the Trinity,
confessing the Three,
with faith in the One
as I face my Maker.

Domini est salus.
Domini est salus.
Domini est salus.
Salus tua, Domine, sit semper vobiscum.

Anon

Cynewulf
8th or 9th century

Elene

Thus miraculously have I, being old and ready to go because
of this fickle carcass, gleaned and woven the craft of words
... I was soiled by my deeds, shackled by my sins, harassed by
cares, and bound and oppressed by bitter worries before the
mighty King granted me knowledge in lucid form as solace
to an old man, meted out his flawless grace and instilled it in
my mind, revealed its radiance, at times augmented it,
unshackled my body, laid open my heart – and unlocked the
art of poesy, which I have used joyously and with a will in
the world.

Amergin

I am the wind which breathes upon the sea,
I am the wave of the ocean,
I am the murmur of the billows,
I am the ox of the seven combats,

I am the vulture upon the rocks,
I am a beam of the sun,
I am the fairest of plants,
I am a wild boar in valour,
I am a salmon in the water,
I am a lake in the plain,
I am a word of science,
I am the point of the lance in battle,
I am the God who creates in the head the fire.
Who is it who throws light into the meeting on the mountain?
Who announces the ages of the moon?
Who teaches the place where couches the sun?

Anon

from **The Dream of the Rood**

8th or 9th century

The rood (the cross) describes the Crucifixion.

I saw the Lord of Mankind
hasten with such courage to climb upon me.
I dared not bow or break there
Against my Lord's wish, when I saw the surface
Of the earth tremble. I could have felled
All my foes, yet I stood firm.
Then the young warrior, God Almighty,
Stripped Himself, firm and unflinching. He climbed
Upon the cross, brave before many, to redeem mankind.
I quivered when the hero clasped me,
Yet I dared not bow to the ground,
Fall to the earth. I had to stand firm.

Anon

Christ and Satan
9th(?) century

Satan's lament after his fall:

'Alas! The majesty of the Lord. Alas! The Protector of the
heavenly hosts. Alas! The might of the ordaining Lord. Alas!
The middle earth. Alas! The bright day. Alas! The joy of God.
Alas! The throng of the angels. Alas! The heaven on high.
Alas! That I am utterly dispossessed of everlasting joy, that I
may not reach up my hands to heaven nor may I look
upwards with my eyes, nor indeed shall I ever hear with my
ears the sound of the clearest trumpet.'

Anon

from The Phoenix
late 9th or 10th century

Those woods
Are lined with bending branches dipping down
Perfect fruit, and nothing pales
Or lessens in that beautiful, holy spot.
No dusk-red, autumn blossoms drift
To the ground, stripping loveliness out of
Wonderful trees, but the heavy boughs
Blossom eternally ripe, always
Green and fresh, exultant ornaments
Dotted upon that brightest plain
By Holy Hands. Nothing breaks
The shape of beauty where the immortal fragrance
Hangs over the land. And so it will stand
As in the beginning He made it, enduring until
The end of time and this earth.

And all
That loveliness surrounds a single, beautiful
Bird, watching over the wood
And his home with strong-feathered wings. His name
Is Phoenix. Death can never follow him
Into that happy land for as long
As the world spins round. In the morning, there,
They say he faces the east and the coming
Sun, peering with eager eyes
At the sea gleaming with the shining brightness
Of God's eternal, jewel-like candle,
The noblest star of all swinging
Slowly aloft, a radiant emblem
Of our Father's ancient work. The glittering
Stars are swallowed in the swelling motion
Of waves rolling out of the west,
Quenched by the dawn as darkness is snuffed
Into vanishing night. And then the noble
Phoenix stares over the water to where
The lamp of Heaven glides out of the sea.

Anon

St Symeon
949–1022

Thy whole Body, pure and divine, blazes with the fire of Thy
divinity, ineffably united to it. Thou has granted, Lord, that
this corruptible temple – my human flesh – be united to Thy
holy flesh, that my blood mingle with Thine; from
henceforth I am a transparent and translucid member of Thy
body.

Ordinary Graces

I know that the Immovable comes down;
I know that the Invisible appears to me;
I know that he who is far outside the whole creation
Takes me unto himself and hides me in his arms.

I know that I shall not die, for I am within the Life,
I have the whole of Life springing up as a fountain within
    me.
He is in my heart, he is in heaven.

4

From St Anselm to Thomas à Kempis:
11th–15th century

St Anselm
1033–1109

Lord, if thou art not here, where shall I seek thee, being absent? But if thou art everywhere, why do I not see thee present? Truly thou dwellest in unapproachable light. But where is unapproachable light, or how shall I come to it? Or who shall lead me to that light and into it, that I may see thee in it? Again, by what marks, under what form, shall I seek thee? I have never seen thee, O Lord, my God; I do not know thy form. What, O most high Lord, shall this man do, an exile far from thee? What shall thy servant do, anxious in his love of thee, and cast out afar from thy face? He pants to see thee, and thy face is too far from him. He longs to come to thee, and thy dwelling-place is inaccessible. He is eager to find thee, and knows not thy place. He desires to seek thee, and does not know thy face. Lord, thou art my God, and thou art my Lord, and never have I seen thee. It is thou that hast made me, and hast made me anew, and hast bestowed upon me all the blessings I enjoy; and not yet do I know thee. Finally, I was created to see thee, and not yet have I done that for which I was made . . .

And thou too, O Lord, how long? How long, O Lord, dost thou forget us; how long dost thou turn thy face from us? When wilt thou look upon us, and hear us? When wilt thou enlighten our eyes, and show us thy face? When wilt thou restore thyself to us? Look upon us, Lord; hear us, enlighten us, reveal thyself to us. Restore thyself to us, that it may be well with us, – thyself, without whom it is so ill with us. Pity our toilings and strivings toward thee, since we can do nothing without thee. Thou dost invite us; do thou help us. I beseech thee, O Lord, that I may not lose hope in sighs, but may breathe anew in hope. Lord, my heart is made bitter by its desolation; sweeten thou it, I beseech thee, with thy consolation. Lord, in hunger I began to seek thee; I beseech thee that I may not cease to hunger for thee. In hunger I have come to thee; let me not go unfed. I have come in poverty to the Rich, in misery to the Compassionate; let me not return empty and despised. And if, before I eat, I sigh, grant, even after sighs, that which I may eat. Lord, I am bowed down and can only look downward; raise me up that I may look upward. My iniquities have gone over my head; they overwhelm me; and, like a heavy load, they weigh me down. Free me from them; unburden me, that the pit of iniquities may not close over me.

Be it mine to look up to thy light, even from afar, even from the depths. Teach me to seek thee, and reveal thyself to me, when I seek thee, for I cannot seek thee, except thou teach me, nor find thee, except thou reveal thyself. Let me seek thee in longing, let me long for thee in seeking; let me find thee in love, and love thee in finding. Lord, I acknowledge and I thank thee that thou hast treated me in this thine image, in order that I may be mindful of thee, may conceive of thee, and love thee; but that image has been so consumed and wasted away by vices, and obscured by the smoke of wrong-doing, that it cannot achieve that for which it was made, except thou renew it, and create it anew. I do not endeavor, O Lord, to penetrate thy sublimity, for in no wise do I compare my understanding with that; but I long to understand in some degree thy truth, which my heart believes and loves. For I do not seek to understand that I may believe, but I believe in order to understand. For this also I believe, – that unless I believed, I should not understand.

Proslogion

Bernard of Clairvaux
1091–1153

Bear with my foolishness for a little, for I want to tell you, as I promised, how these things took place in me. This is indeed of no importance; I put myself forward only in order to be useful to you, and if you are helped I am consoled for my egoism; if not, I shall have exhibited my folly. I confess, then, to speak foolishly, that the Word has visited me – indeed, very often. But, though He has frequently come into my soul, I have never at any time been aware of the moment of His coming. I have felt Him, but never have I felt His coming or departure ... It is not by the eyes that He enters, for He has no colour; nor by the ears, for His coming is silent; nor by the nostrils, for He is blended with the mind, and not with the air; nor again does He enter by the mouth, for His nature cannot be eaten or drunk; nor lastly can we trace Him by touch, for He is intangible ...

You will ask then how, since His track is thus traceless, I could know that He is present? Because He is living and full of energy, and as soon as He has entered me, has quickened my sleeping soul, and aroused, softened and goaded my heart, which was torpid and hard as a stone. He has begun to pluck up and destroy, plant and build, to water the dry places, light up the dark places, throw open what was shut, inflame with warmth what was cold, straighten the crooked path and make rough places smooth ... In the reformation and renewal of the spirit of my mind, that is my inward man, I have seen something of the loveliness of His beauty, and meditating on these things have been filled with wonder at the multitude of His greatness.

But when the Word withdrew, all these spiritual powers and faculties began to droop and languish, as if the fire were taken from beneath a bubbling pot; and this is to me the sign of His departure. Then my soul must needs be sad and sorry, till He comes back and my heart again warms within me as it is wont; for this is to me the sign that He has returned.

Sermons on the Canticles

Jesu Dulcis Memoria
late 12th century

I'll call for Jesus on my bed
From the locked chamber of my heart.
In privacy and public place
I'll shout for him with earnest cry.

With Mary when the dawn grows light,
I'll call for Jesus at the tomb;
With clamor of the heart I'll cry
I'll quest with soul and not with eye.

Anon

St Aelred of Rievaulx
1110–1167

What, O my God, is love? It is, if I mistake not, that spiritual, astonishing delight, so pleasant because so pure, its very gentleness the measure of its genuineness, bestowing gladness proportionate to its greatness. It is the heart's palate that tastes you, so pleasant; the eye that glimpses you, who are so kind and gracious; the place that enfolds you, the Infinite.

Mirror of Charity

Who love you, find their rest in you; true rest, tranquillity, peace, the soul's very Sabbath.

Mirror of Charity

Sadness in Spring
13th century

Maytime, loveliest season,
Loud bird-parley, new growth green,
Ploughs in furrow, oxen yoked,
Emerald sea, land-hues dappled.

When cuckoos call from fair tree-tops
Greater grows my sorrow;
Stinging smoke, grief awake
For my kinsfolk's passing.

On hill, in vale, in ocean's isles.
Whichever way man goes,
Blest Christ there's no evading.

Welsh, Anon

Mechthild of Magdeburg
1207–1282/97

God Speaks to the Soul

And God said to the soul:
I desired you before the world began.
I desire you now
As you desire me.
And where the desires of two come together
There love is perfected.

How the Soul Speaks to God

Lord, you are my lover,
My longing,
My flowing stream,
My sun,
And I am your reflection.

How God Answers the Soul

It is my nature that makes me love you often,
For I am love itself.
It is my longing that makes me love you intensely,
For I yearn to be loved from the heart.
It is my eternity that makes me love you long,
For I have no end.

Hadewijch of Antwerp
13th century

All things
are too small
to hold me,
I am so vast

In the Infinite
I reach
for the Uncreated

I have
touched it,
it undoes me
wider than wide

Everything else
is too narrow

You know this well,
you who are also there

Jacopone da Todi
c. 1228/30–1306

Of Differences in the Contemplation of the Cross
(A Dialogue between Two Brothers in Religion)

(First Brother speaks)
I flee the Cross that doth my heart devour,
I cannot bear its ardour and its power.

I cannot bear this great and dreadful heat;
Far from the Cross, from Love, on flying feet
I haste away; my heart at every beat
   Consumes me with that burning memory.

(Second Brother)
Brother, why dost thou flee from this delight?
This is the joy I yearn for, day and night:
Brother, this is but weakness in my sight,
   To flee from joy and peace so cravenly.
. . .

(First Brother)
Ah, thou art warmed; but I am in the Fire:
Thine the delight, and mine the flaming Pyre;
I cannot breathe within this furnace dire!
   Thou hast not entered There, It burns not thee.

(Second Brother)
Brother, thy words I cannot understand:
Why dost thou flee from gentle Love's demand?
Tell my thy state, and let me take thy hand,
   The while I listen to this mystery!

(First Brother)
Brother, thou breath'st the perfume of the Wine;
But I have drunk It, and no strength of mine
Can bear the onslaught of that Must Divine,
   That ruthless, ceaseth not to torture me!

                       Lauda LXXV

Ramón Lull
*c.*1233–*c.*1315

Far above Love is the Beloved; far beneath it is the Lover; and Love, which lies between these two, made the Beloved to descend to the Lover, and the Lover to rise toward the Beloved. And this ascending and descending is the being and the life of Love – of that Love which makes the Lover to endure pain and which ever serves the Beloved.

On the right side of Love stands the Beloved, and on the left side is the Lover; and thus he cannot reach the Beloved unless he pass through Love. And before Love stands the Beloved, and beyond is the Lover; so that the Lover cannot reach Love unless his thoughts and desires have first passed through the Beloved.

The Book of the Lover and the Beloved

Angela of Foligno
1248–1309

At one time I was meditating on the great sufferings of our Lord Jesus Christ on the Cross and thought especially of the nails which I had heard were of the sort that caused the flesh of the hands and feet to be driven into the wood. I wanted to see those little pieces of flesh that the nails had driven so violently into the wood. Then I felt so immensely grieved because of Christ's pain that I could not stand any longer on my feet and I sat on the ground. Then I beheld Christ inclining his head upon my arms which I had stretched out on the ground. He showed me his throat and his arms and at once my grief was transformed into joy, a joy so over-whelming and different from all other joys that I did not see

[50]

or feel anything else. The beauty of that throat was something most wonderful and ineffable and I perceived that his
beauty proceeded from his divinity.

He did not show me anything else except that most
comely throat, most gracious to behold, the beauty of which
cannot be likened to anything else or to any colour in the
world, except that it seemed to me like the clearness of
Christ's body, which I see sometimes at the elevation of the
Host.

Visions, Revelations and Teachings of Angela of Foligno

Meister Eckhart
1260–1327

God is a sheer absolute one, sundered from all two-ness, and
in whom we must eternally sink from nothingness to
nothingness.

The eye in which I see God is the same eye in which God
sees me. My eye and God's eye are one eye and one seeing,
one knowing and one loving.

Sermons

Dante Alighieri
1265–1321

from Paradiso

O radiance of God, through which I saw
the noble triumph of the true realm, give
to me the power to speak of what I saw!
　　Above, on high, there is a light that makes
apparent the Creator to the creature
whose only peace lies in his seeing Him.

Richard Rolle

1300–1349

In the beginning truly of my conversion and singular purpose I thought I would be like the little bird that for love of its lover longs; but in her longing she is gladdened when he comes that she loves. And joying she sings, and singing she longs, but in sweetness and heat. It is said the nightingale to song and melody all night is given, that she may please him to whom she is joined. How mickle more with greatest sweetness to Christ my Jesu should I sing, that is spouse of my soul, by all this present life that is night in regard of clearness to come.

The Fire of Love

Jesu, my Lord, mine own sweeting,
Hold me ever in Thy keeping;
Make of me Thine own darling,
That I love Thee above all thing.

. . .

Jesu, if Thou from me dost go,
Mine heart is full of pain and woe;
What may I say but 'Well-a-woe!'
When Thou, my Sweet, art gone me fro'?

Jesu, my Life, my Lord, my King!
To thee my soul hath great longing;
Thou has wedded it with Thy ring;
When thy will is, to Thee it bring!

John Tauler
*c.*1300–1361

When the hart has eluded the hounds and reached water he gives himself up to quenching his thirst at his ease. Man, when with Divine help he has shaken off the rabble of dogs, big and little, and reached God, does the same: he drinks at the sacred fountain till he is filled and intoxicated with God, and in the fullness of his happiness forgets himself completely. Then does it seem to him that he could work miracles, pass through fire and water and massed swords, face death itself; he fears neither life nor death, pleasure nor pain. In this state of exultation sometimes he weeps, sometimes sings, sometimes laughs.

Then the rationalists come along. They know nothing of the marvellous works which the Holy Spirit can do on His own, for they can recognize nothing beyond the gifts of nature. And they say, 'Good Lord! How worked up and excited you are!' . . . But the lovers of God pass into a wordless peace, where all is happiness and joy; whatever happens to them, whatever they do, that joy and peace remain, the flames of love leap within them, and the heat makes their heart boil over with happiness.

Sermon for the Monday before Palm Sunday

Henry Suso
1300–1365

The Disciple said: Yet I see that there are mountains and valleys and water and air, all kinds of created things: how then canst Thou say there is but One?

The Pure Word answered and said thus: I will tell thee more: unless man can understand two contraries, that is, two contradictory things, together, then truly and without any doubt it is not easy to speak to him of such things For, until he understands this, he has not yet started out on the path of the life that I am talking about.

Question: What are these contraries?

Answer: An eternal Nothing and the creation in time.

Question: Two contraries in one are in every respect a negation of all knowledge.

Answer: I and thou do not meet on one branch or at one place; thou goest one way and I another. Thy questions proceed from human reason, and I reply from the reason that is above all human understanding. Thou must become ignorant if thou wouldst attain it, for by ignorance the truth is known.

Little Book of Truth

Rulman Merswin
1310–1382

And the overwhelming joy made him ill. The man thought to himself and said: 'Who are you that you should be filled with such overwhelming joy?' He sat for a long while in thought, and the more he thought the less he could understand what had happened. Then he decided to write about these things as he had been commanded. But all his senses and reason could not express what he had seen; no words could describe it. Then he thought of expressing it in pictures and formulas; but again he could not, for it was beyond all pictures and formulas. Then he thought he would reason about it and reach by reason and concepts. The more he thought about it the less he knew, because it was greater than anything he had ever seen or heard of. This amazed him and he said: 'O Beloved, tell me what thou meanest. Thou saidst I had to see the origin and then write about it so that men could conceive it. Now thou hadst made me see such a great wonder that I cannot express it in words. I have tried with all my reason, but no word will describe it. Nor can I describe where I have been or what I have seen and heard except for one thing: that I know my heart and my soul are full of an overwhelming joy which frightens me, for I know it will be hard to control.'

The answer came: 'You must do it as far as you can, because men nowadays refuse the divine gifts, not knowing what they are.'

Book of the Nine Rocks

The Cloud of Unknowing
14th century

For in the beginning it is usual to feel nothing but a kind of darkness about your mind, or as it were, a cloud of unknowing. You will seem to know nothing and to feel nothing except a naked intent toward God in the depths of your being. Try as you might, this darkness and this cloud will remain between you and your God. You will feel frustrated, for your mind will be unable to grasp him, and your heart will not relish the delight of his love. But learn to be at home in this darkness. Return to it as often as you can, letting your spirit cry out to him whom you love. For if, in this life, you hope to feel and see God as he is in himself it must be within this darkness and this cloud. But if you strive to fix your love on him forgetting all else, which is the work of contemplation I have urged you to begin, I am confident that God in his goodness will bring you to a deep experience of himself.

For of all other creatures and their works – yea, and of the works of God Himself – may a man through grace have fulness of knowing, and well can he think of them; but of God

Himself can no man think. And therefore I would leave all that thing that I can think, and choose to my love that thing that I cannot think. For why, he may well be loved, but not thought. By love may he be gotten and holden; but by thought never.

Anon

Julian of Norwich
c. 1343–*c.* 1420

And thus I saw Him, and sought Him: and I had Him, and I wanted Him.

Revelations of Divine Love

In this same time Our Lord showed me a ghostly sight of His homely loving.

I saw that He is to us everything that is good and comfortable for us. He is our clothing that for love wrappeth us, claspeth us, and all becloseth us for tender love, that He may never leave us; being to us all thing that is good, as to mine understanding.

Also in this he showed [me] a little thing, the quantity of a hazel-nut in the palm of my hand; and it was as round as a ball. I looked thereupon with eye of my understanding, and thought: 'What may this be?' And it was generally answered thus: 'It is all that is made.' I marvelled how it might last, for methought it might suddenly have fallen to naught for littleness. And I was answered in my understanding: 'It lasteth, and ever shall [last] for that God loveth it.' And so all thing hath Being by the love of God.

In this little thing, I saw three properties. The first is that God made it; the second is that God loveth it; the third is that God keepeth it. But what is to me soothly the Maker, the Keeper, and the Lover – I cannot tell; for till I am substantially oned [united] to Him, I may never have full rest nor very bliss; that is to say, till I be so fastened to Him, that there is right naught that is made betwixt my God and me.

Revelations of Divine Love

All shall be well, and all shall be well, and all manner of things shall be well.

Revelations of Divine Love

Margery Kempe
*c.*1373–*c.*1439

... she heard a sound of melody so sweet and delectable, that she thought she had been in Paradise, and therewith she started out of her bed and said: 'Alas that ever I did sin! It is full merry in Heaven.' This melody was so sweet that it surpassed all melody that ever might be heard in this world, without any comparison, and caused her, when she heard any mirth or melody afterwards, to have full plenteous and abundant tears of high devotion, with great sobbings and sighings after the bliss of Heaven, not dreading the shames and spites of this wretched world.

The Book of Margery Kempe

Quia Amore Langueo
14th or 15th century

In the vale of restless mind
I sought in mountain and in mead,
Trusting a true love for to find,
Upon an hill then took I heed;
A voice I heard – and near I yede –

In huge dolour, complaining tho:
'See, dear soul, my sides bleed,
Quia amore langueo.'

Under this mount I found a tree;
Under this tree a man sitting;
From head to foot wounded was he,
His heart-blood I saw bleeding;
A seemly man to be a king
A gracious face to look unto.
I asked him how he had been paining.
He said: '*Quia amore langueo.*

'I am true love that false was never:
My sister, man's soul, I loved her thus;
Because I would on no wise dissever,
I left my kingdom glorious;
I purveyed her a place full precious;
She flit, I followed; I loved her so
That I suffered these pains piteous,
Quia amore langueo.

'My fair love and my spouse bright,
I saved her from beating and she hath me bet;
I clothed her in grace and heavenly light,
This bloody source she hath on me set.
For longing love I will not let;
Sweet strokes be these, lo!
I have loved her ever as I het,
Quia amore langueo.

'I crowned her with bliss, and she me with thorn;
I led her to chamber and she me to die;

I brought her to worship, and she me to scorn;
I did her reverence, and she me villainy.
To love that loveth is no maistry;
Her hate made never my love her foe;
Ask then no mo questions why,
Quia amore langueo.

'Look into mine hands, man!
These gloves were given me when I her sought;
They be not white, but red and wan,
Embroidered with blood, my spouse them bought;
They will not off, I leave them nought,
I woo her with them wherever she go;
These hands ful friendly for her fought,
Quia amore langueo.

'Marvel not, man, though I sit still;
My love hath shod me wonder strait;
She buckled my feet as was her will,
With sharp nails – well thou mayst wait!
In my love was never deceit,
For all my members I have opened her to;
My body I made her heart's bait,
Quia amore langueo.

'In my side I have made a nest;
Look in me how wide a wound is here!
This is her chamber, here shall she rest,
That she and I may sleep in fere.
Here may she wash, if any filth were,
Here is succour for all her woe;
Come if she will, she shall have cheer,
Quia amore langueo.

'I will abide till she be ready,
I will her sue if she say nay;
If she be reckless, I will be ready,
If she be dangerous, I will her pray.
If she do weep, then bid I nay;
Mine arms be spread to clip her to;
Cry once: I come. Now, soul, assay!
Quia amore langueo.

'I sit on an hill for to see far,
I look to the bale; my spouse I see:
Now runs she awayward, now comes she nearer,
Yet from my eye-sight she may not be.
Some wait their prey to make her flee;
I run tofore to chastise her foe.
Recover, my soul, again to me,
Quia amore langueo.

'My sweet spouse, will we go play?
Apples be ripe in my garden;
I shall clothe thee in new array,
Thy meat shall be milk, honey and wine.
Now, dear soul, let us go dine,
Thy sustenance is in my scrippe, lo!
Tarry not now, fair spouse mine,
Quia amore langueo.

'If thou be foul, I shall make thee clean;
If thou be sick, I shall thee heal,
If thou aught mourn, I shall bemene.
Spouse, why wilt thou nought with me deal?
Thou foundest never love so leal;
What wilt thou, soul, that I shall do?
I may of unkindness thee appeal,
Quia amore langueo.

'What shall I do now with my spouse?
Abide I will her gentleness.
Would she look once out of her house
Of fleshly affections and uncleanness,
Her bed is made, her bolster is bliss,
Her chamber is chosen, such are no mo.
Look out at the windows of kindness,
Quia amore langueo.

'Long and love thou never so high,
Yet is my love more than thine may be;
Thou gladdest, thou weepest, I sit thee by;
Yet might thou, spouse, look once at me!
Spouse, should I always feed thee
With child's meat? Nay, love, not so!
I prove thy love with adversity,
Quia amore langueo.

'My spouse is in chamber, hold your peace;
Make no noise, but let her sleep.
My babe shall suffer no disease,
I may not hear my dear child weep;
For with my pap I shall her keep.
No wonder though I tend her to:
This hole in my side had never been so deep,
But *quia amore langueo.*

'Wax not weary, mine own dear wife:
What meed is aye to live in comfort?
For in tribulation I run more rife
Oftentimes than in disport;
In wealth, in woe, ever I support,
Then, dear soul, go never me fro!
Thy meed is marked, when thou art mort,
Quia amore langueo.'   *Anon*

Thomas à Kempis
1380–1471

You cannot escape it, whithersoever you run. For where-soever you go you carry yourself with you, and shall always find yourself. Turn upwards or turn downwards, turn inwards or turn outwards: everywhere, you shall find the cross.

Imitation of Christ

5

From Martin Luther to
Ben Jonson:
15th–16th century

Martin Luther
1483–1546

I greatly longed to understand Paul's Epistle to the Romans
and nothing stood in the way but that one expression, 'the
justice of God', because I took it to mean that justice where-
by God is just and deals justly in punishing the unjust. My
situation was that, although an impeccable monk, I stood
before God as a sinner troubled in conscience, and I had no
confidence that my merit would assuage him. Therefore I
did not love a just and angry God, but rather hated and
murmured against him. Yet I clung to the dear Paul and had
a great yearning to know what he meant.

Night and day I pondered until I saw the connection
between the justice of God and the statement that 'the just
shall live by his faith'. Then I grasped that the justice of God
is that righteousness by which through grace and sheer
mercy God justifies us through faith. Thereupon I felt myself
to be reborn and to have gone through open doors into
paradise. The whole of Scripture took on a new meaning,
and whereas before the 'justice of God' had filled me with
hate, now it became to me inexpressibly sweet in greater
love. This passage of Paul became to me a gate to heaven.

Here I Stand

Myles Coverdale
1488–1568

... such grace and glory is inwardly seen with the eyes of faith, and felt in the spirit, being hid here in time in the shape of the cross. For Christ doth not straightway by and by declare himself openly unto Mary Magdalene, as he is in his glory; but standeth there as a gardener, and speaketh unto her, by the which voice she knoweth him: he long deferreth the comfort, permitting her a good while to weep and lament, that the joy and consolation afterward may be the greater. But the cause why he so long delayeth his help and comfort from these that be his own is, that their inward desires may be the more fervent and earnest, and that he may stir up and kindle their faith, then cometh he with his comfort.

Fruitful Lessons: Of the Resurrection of Christ

St Ignatius Loyola
1491–1556

One day St Ignatius went to pray in a church outside Manresa. The road led along a river bank. When he sat down to rest, his eyes fixed on the running water and his mind in prayer, he experienced an intense and sudden enlightenment. Although he could never find words to describe what had been revealed to him there, he used to say that all things seemed to have been made new, and that what he understood in that moment exceeded everything that he had learned during his whole life.

St Teresa of Avila
1515–1582

A much greater love for and confidence in this Lord began to develop in me when I saw him as one with whom I could converse so continually. I saw that he was man, even though he was God; that he wasn't surprised by human weaknesses; that he understands our miserable make-up, subject to many falls on account of the first sin which he came to repair. I can speak with him as with a friend, even though he is Lord.

The Book of Her Life

Not long afterwards, his Majesty began, according to his promise, to make it clear that it was He Himself who appeared, by the growth in me of the love of God so strong, that I knew not who could have infused it; for it was most supernatural, and I had not attained to it by any efforts of my own. I saw myself dying with a desire to see God, and I knew not how to seek that life otherwise than by dying. Certain great impetuosities of love, though not so intolerable as those of which I have spoken before, nor yet of so great worth, overwhelmed me. I knew not what to do; for nothing gave me pleasure, and I had no control over myself. Oh, supreme artifice of our Lord! How tenderly didst Thou deal with thy miserable slave! How didst Thou hide Thyself from me and didst yet constrain me with Thy love, with a death so sweet that my soul would never wish it over.

The Book of Her Life

Luis de León
1528–1591

The Heavenly Life

Dear Love, did I but know
The pasture where Thy noontide rest would be,
I'd break my toils below,
And never stray from Thee,
But with Thy flock remain, for ever free.

St John of the Cross
1542–1591

Other verses with a divine meaning
by the same author

Not without hope did I ascend
Upon an amorous quest to fly
And up I soared so high, so high,
I seized my quarry in the end.

    . . .

The more I rose into the height
More dazzled, blind, and lost I spun.
The greatest conquest ever won
I won in blindness, like the night.
Because love urged me on my way
I gave that mad, blind, reckless leap
That soared me up so high and steep
That in the end I seized my prey.

The steeper upward that I flew
On so vertiginous a quest

The humbler and more lowly grew
My spirit, fainting in my breast.
I said, 'None yet can find the way'
But as my spirit bowed more low,
Higher and higher did I go
Till in the end I seized my prey.

By such strange means did I sustain
A thousand starry flights in one,
Since hope of Heaven yet by none
Was ever truly hoped in vain.
Only by hope I won my way
Nor did my hope my aim belie,
Since I soared up so high, so high,
That in the end I seized my prey.

Translated by Roy Campbell

Night of Sense

When they [spiritual persons] are going about these spiritual
exercises with increasing delight and pleasure, and when they
think the sun of Divine favour is shining on them more
brightly, God turns all this light they are enjoying into darkness, and shuts against them the door and the source of the
fresh spiritual water which they were tasting in God when-
soever and for as long as they desired. (For as they were weak
and tender, no door was closed to them, as St John says in
the Apocalypse, iii, 8.)

He leaves them, then, completely in darkness, so much so
that with their sensible imagination and meditation they
know not where to betake themselves. For they can make no
progress in meditation, as they were in the habit of doing
before, their inward senses being overwhelmed by this night,

and left in a state of such aridity that not only do they experience no pleasure and consolation in the spiritual things and good exercises in which they were accustomed to find their delight and pleasure, but, on the contrary, they find these things insipid and bitter. For, as I have said, God sees that they have grown a little, and are becoming strong enough to lay aside their swaddling clothes. So He takes them from His gentle breast, sets them down from His arms and teaches them to walk on their own feet. This makes them feel very strange, and they think everything is going wrong with them.

Dark Night of the Soul

from Songs between the soul and the bridegroom

BRIDE
My Beloved is the mountains,
And lonely wooded valleys,
Strange islands,
And resounding rivers,
The whistling of love-stirring breezes,

The tranquil night
At the time of the rising dawn,
Silent music,
Sounding solitude,
The supper that refreshes, and deepens love.

The Spiritual Canticle

The father only spoke but once: it was his Word. He spoke it eternally and in eternal silence. It is in silence that the ear will hear it.

Sayings of Light and Love

St Alonso (Rodriguez), the Doorkeeper
late 16th century

Once when St Alonso was engaged in earnestly praying that he might be granted joy in suffering and love his persecutors, he had the following experience: Suddenly, before he realised what was happening, there came upon him a sort of fiery comet, like those which fall from heaven at night. It came down on him from on high and wounded him in the side so that it left his heart on fire for his neighbour. And it seemed to him that he could not wish ill towards his neighbour, even if he were to do the most terrible things.

St Alonso, on hearing the door-bell, would raise up his heart to God and exclaim: Lord, I shall open the door for you, for love of you! As he hurried to answer it he would feel as glad as if it really was God he was going to let in, and he would say: I'm coming Lord! When someone rang loudly and impatiently, his natural reaction was to get upset, but he mastered this feeling and by the time he had reached the door he had calmed down and he opened it as if the caller had given only a gentle ring. No matter who the caller might be, it seemed to him that he was opening the door to his God.

Autobiography

Lope Felix de Vega Carpio
1562–1635

To-morrow

Lord, what am I, that, with unceasing care,
Thou didst seek after me? that Thou didst wait,
Wet with unhealthy dews, before my gate,
And pass the gloomy nights of winter there?

Oh, strange delusion, that I did not greet
Thy blessed approach! and oh! to heaven how lost,
If my ingratitude's unkindly frost,
Has chilled the bleeding wounds upon Thy feet!

How oft my guardian angel gently cried,
'Soul, from thy casement look, and thou shalt see
How He persists to knock and wait for thee!'
And, oh! how often to that voice of sorrow,
'To-morrow we will open,' I replied;
and when to-morrow came, I answered still, 'To-morrow.'

Translated by Henry Wadsworth Longfellow

Ben Jonson
1572/3–1637

A Hymn to God the Father

Hear me, O God!
A broken heart
Is my best part:
Use still thy rod,
That I may prove
Therein, thy love.

If thou hadst not
Been stern to me
But left me free,
I had forgot
Myself and thee.

For sin's so sweet,
As minds ill bent
Rarely repent,

Until they meet
Their punishment:

Who more can crave
Than thou hast done:
Thou gav'st a son,
To free a slave?
First made of nought;
With all since bought.

Sin, Death and Hell,
His glorious Name
Quite overcame;
Yet I rebel,
And slight the same.

But I'll come in,
Before my loss,
Me farther toss,
As sure to win
Under His Cross.

6

From Marina of Escobar to Cotton Mather:
16th–18th century

The Thief

'Say bold but blessed thief,
That in a trice
Slipped into paradise,
And in plaine day
Stol'st heaven awaye,
What trick couldst thou invent
To compass thy intent?
What arms?
What charms?'
'Love and belief.'

'Say bold but blessed thief,
How couldst thou read
A crown upon that head?
What text, what gloss,
A kingdom on a cross?
How couldst thou come to spy
God in a man to die?
What light?
What sight?'
'The sight of grief –

'I sight to God his pain;
And by that sight
I saw the light;
Thus did my grief
Beget relief.
And take this rule from me,
Pity thou him, he'll pity thee.
Use this,
Ne'er miss,
Heaven may be stol'n again.'

Anon

Marina of Escobar
1554–1633

Then He led me into the heavenly Jerusalem. I saw a table, spread as for a feast; the splendour cannot be described. I saw many elect citizens of heaven sit down at this table – the secret spiritual food refreshing and strengthening innumerable spirits was God Himself. I saw a thousand other things and wondered much. I remarked specially some beautiful little dogs running about the festive table and joyfully eating the crumbs falling from it. It was God Himself who in the shape of crumbs came down to feed and make glad these little creatures. At His command an angel decorated each with a collar of flowers. It was revealed to me that the little dogs symbolized the contemplative souls still on earth who also are fed by this heavenly food, because they hunger only to know God, and have renounced the pleasures of earth.

Lancelot Andrewes
1555–1626

Sermon on the Nativity, Christmas 1622

There now remains nothing but to include ourselves, and bear our part with them [the Magi], and with the Angels, and all who on this day adored Him.

This was the load-star of the Magi, and what were they? They were gentiles. So are we. But if it must be ours, then we are to go with them; *vade, et fac similitur,* 'Go and do likewise' (Luke 10:37). It is *stella gentium,* but *idem agentium,* 'the gentiles' star,' but 'such gentiles as overtake these and keep company with them.' In their *dicentes,* 'confessing their faith freely'; in their *vidimus,* 'grounding it thoroughly'; in their *venimus,* 'hasting to come to Him speedily'; in their *ubi est?* 'enquiring Him out diligently'; and in their *adorare Eum,* 'worshipping Him devoutly', *per omnia,* doing as these did; worshipping and thus worshipping, celebrating and thus celebrating the feast of His birth.

We cannot say *vidimus stellam*; the star is long gone since, not now to be seen. Yet I hope for all that, that *venimus adorare,* 'we be come thither to worship'. It will be the more acceptable, if not seeing it we worship though. It is enough we read of it in the text; we see it there. And indeed, as I said, it skills not for the star in the firmament, if the same Day-Star be risen in our hearts that was in theirs, and the same beams of it to be seen, all five. For then we have our part in it no less, nay full out as much as they. And it will bring us whither it brought them, to Christ. Who, at His second appearing in glory shall call forth these wise men, and all that have ensued the steps of their faith, and that upon the reason specified in the text; for I have seen their star shining and showing forth itself by the like beams: and as they came to worship Me, so am I come to do them worship. A *venite* then, for a *venimus* now. Their star I have seen, and give them a place above among the stars. They fell down: I will lift them up, and exalt them. And as they offered to Me, so am I come to bestow on them, and to reward them with the endless joy and bliss of My Heavenly Kingdom.

Sermons

St Francis de Sales
1567–1622

Even human lovers are content, sometimes, with being near or within sight of the person they love without speaking to her, and without even distinctly thinking of her or her perfections, satiated, as it were, and satisfied to relish this dear presence, not by any reflection they make upon it, but by a certain gratification and repose, which their spirit takes in it . . .

Now this repose sometimes goes so deep in its tranquillity, that the whole soul and all its powers fall as it were asleep, and make no movement nor action whatever except the will alone, and even this does no more than receive the delight and satisfaction which the presence of the well-beloved affords. And what is yet more admirable is, that the will does not even perceive the delight and contentment which she receives, enjoying insensibly, being not mindful of herself, but of Him whose presence gives her this pleasure, as happens frequently when, surprised by a light slumber, we only hear indistinctly what our friends are saying around us, or feel their caresses almost imperceptibly, not feeling that we feel.

John Donne
1572–1631

Batter my heart, three-person'd God, for you
As yet but knock, breathe, shine, and seek to mend;
That I may rise, and stand, o'erthrow me, and bend
Your force, to breake, blowe, burn and make me new.
I, like an usurpt towne, to another due,
Labour to admit you, but Oh, to no end,
Reason your viceroy in me, me should defend,
But is captiv'd, and proves weake or untrue.
Yet dearely I love you, and would be loved faine,
But am betroth'd unto your enemie:
Divorce me, untie, or breake that knot againe,
Take me to you, imprison me, for I
Except you enthrall me, never shall be free,
Nor ever chaste, except you ravish me.

Francis Quarles
1592–1644

from Wherefore Hidest Thou Thy Face and Holdest Me for Thine Enemy?
(Job XIII, 24)

Why dost thou shade thy lovely face? Oh why
Does that eclipsing hand so long deny
The sunshine of thy soul-enlivening eye?

Without that light, what light remains in me?
Thou art my life, my way, my light; in thee
I live, I move, and by thy beams I see.

Thou art my life: if thou but turn away,
My life's a thousand deaths; thou art my way:
Without thee, Lord, I travel not, but stray.

My light thou art: without thy glorious sight,
My eyes are darkened with perpetual night.
My God, thou art my way, my life, my light.

Thou art my way: I wander, if thou fly:
Thou art my light: if hid, how blind am I!
Thou art my life: if thou withdraw, I die.

My eyes are blind and dark, I cannot see;
To whom, or whither, should my darkness flee,
But to the light? And who's that light but thee?

My path is lost, my wandering steps do stray;
I cannot safely go, nor safely stay;
Whom should I seek but thee, my path, my way?

Oh, I am dead: to whom shall I, poor I,
Repair? To whom shall my sad ashes fly,
But life? And where is life but in thine eye?

And yet thou turn'st away thy face, and fly'st me;
And yet I sue for grace, and thou deny'st me;
Speak, art thou angry, Lord, or only try'st me?

George Herbert
1593–1633

The Search

Whither, O whither art Thou fled,
    My Lord, my Love?
My searches are my daily bread,
    Yet never prove.

My knees pierce the earth, mine eyes the sky;
    And yet the sphere
And centre both to me deny
    That Thou art there.

Yet can I mark how herbs below
    Grow green and gay,
As if to meet Thee they did know
    While I decay.

Yet can I mark how stars above
    Simper and shine,
As having keys unto Thy love,
    While poor I pine.

I sent a sigh to seek Thee out,
    Deep drawn in pain,
Winged like an arrow; but my scout
    Returns in vain.

I turned another – having store –
    Into a groan,
Because the search was dumb before;
    But all was one.

Lord, dost Thou some new fabric mould
    Which favour wins,
And keeps Thee present; leaving the old
    Unto their sins?

Where is my God? what hidden place
    Conceals Thee still?
What covert dare eclipse Thy face?
    Is it Thy will?

O let not that of anything;
    Let rather brass,
Or steel, or mountains be Thy ring,
    And I will pass.

Thy will such an entrenching is,
    As passeth thought:
To it all strength, all subtilties
    Are things of nought.

Thy will such a strange distance is,
    As that to it
East and West touch, the poles do kiss,
    And parallels meet.

Since then my grief must be as large
    As is Thy space,
Thy distance from me; see my charge,
    Lord, see my case.

O take these bars, these lengths, away;
    Turn and restore me:
'Be not Almighty,' let me say,
    'Against but for me.'

When Thou dost turn and wilt be near,
    What edge so keen,
What point so piercing can appear
    To come between?

For as Thy absence doth excel
    All distance known,
So doth Thy nearness bear the bell,
    Making two one.

Matthew Hale
1609–1676

Christmas Day (1659)

But art thou come, dear Saviour? Hath Thy love
Thus made Thee stoop, and leave Thy throne above
The lofty Heavens, and thus Thyself to dress
In dust to visit mortals? Could no less
A condescension serve? And after all,
The mean reception of a cratch and stall?
Dear Lord, I'll fetch Thee hence; I have a room
'Tis poor, but 'tis my best, if thou wilt come
Within so small a cell, where I would fain
Mine and the world's Redeemer entertain;
I mean my heart; 'tis sluttish, I confess,
And will not mend Thy lodging, Lord, unless
Thou send before Thy Harbinger, I mean
Thy pure and purging grace, to make it clean,
And sweep its nasty corners; then I'll try
To wash it also with a weeping eye;
And when 'tis swept and washed, I then will go,
And with Thy leave, I'll fetch some flowers that grow

In Thine own garden, faith, and love to Thee;
With those I'll dress it up; and these shall be
My rosemary and bays; yet when my best
Is done, the room's not fit for such a Guest.
But here is the cure; Thy presence Lord, alone
Will make a stall a court, a cratch a throne.

Anne Bradstreet
1612–1672

I have often been perplexed that I have not found that
constant joy in my pilgrimage and refreshing which I
supposed most of the servants of God have, although He
hath not left me altogether without the witness of His holy
spirit, who hath oft given me His word and set to His seal
that it shall be well with me. I have sometimes tasted of that
hidden manna that the world knows not, and have set up my
Ebeneezer and have resolved with myself that against such a
promise, such tastes of sweetness, the gates of hell shall never
prevail; yet have I many times sinkings and droopings, and
not enjoyed that felicity that sometimes I have done. But
when I have been in darkness and seen no light, yet have I
desired to stay myself upon the Lord and when I have been
in the light of His countenance upon me, although He
ground me to powder, it would be but light to me; yea, oft
have I thought were I in hell itself and could find there the
love of God toward me it would be a heaven. And could I
have been in heaven without the love of God, it would have
been a hell to me, for in truth it is the absence and presence
of God that makes heaven or hell.

Letter

Jeremy Taylor
1613–1667

There is a degree of Meditation so exalted that it changes the very name and is called Contemplation; and it is in the unitive way of religion, that is, it consists in unions and adherences to GOD; it is a prayer of quietness and silence, and a meditation extraordinary, a discourse without variety, a vision and intuition of divine excellences, an immediate entry into an orb of light, and a resolution of all our faculties into sweetnesses, affections, and starings upon the divine beauty; and is carried on to ecstasies, raptures, suspensions, elevations, abstractions, and apprehensions beatifical . . . But this is a thing not to be discoursed of but felt . . . They that pretend to these heights call them the secrets of the kingdom; but they are such which no man can describe; such as GOD hath not revealed in the publication of the gospel; such for the airing of which there are no means prescribed, and to which no man is obliged, and which are not in any man's power to obtain; nor such which it is lawful to pray for or desire . . . If a man be more in love with GOD by such instruments, or more endeared to virtue, or made more severe and watchful in his repentance, it is an excellent gift and grace of GOD . . . But if the person be made unquiet, inconstant, proud, pusillanimous, of high opinion, pertinacious and confident in uncertain judgments, or desperate, it is certain they are temptations and illusions.

Of Meditation

Henry Vaughan
1621–1695

from The Night

There is in God, some say,
A deep but dazzling darkness; as men here
Say it is late and dusky, because they
    See not all clear.
  Oh for that Night! Where I in Him
  Might live invisible and dim!

Blaise Pascal
1623–1662

Amulet *or* Memorial

The year of Grace 1654.
Monday 23 November, feast of St Clement, pope and martyr,
    And of others in the martyrology,
      Eve of St Chrysogonus, martyr, and others,
From about half-past ten in the evening to about half an hour
    after midnight,
      Fire

'God of Abraham, God of Isaac, God of Jacob,'
  not of the philosophers and learned.
Certitude, Certitude, love, joy, peace.
  God of Jesus Christ
  Deum meum et deum vestrum.
  Thy God shall be my God.'
  Forgetfulness of the world and of everything outside God.
He is not found except by the means taught in the Gospel.
  Greatness of the human soul

'Holy Father, the world hath not known Thee, but I have
known Thee.'

Joy, Joy, Joy, tears of joy.

I am separated from Him.

Dereliquerunt me fontem aquae vivae. [They have forsaken me,
the fountain of living water. Jer. ii.13]

My God, wilt Thou leave me?

Let me not be eternally separated from Him.

'This is eternal life, that they know Thee the only true God
and Jesus Christ whom Thou hast sent.'

      Jesus Christ

      Jesus Christ

I am separated from Him; I have shunned, renounced, crucified
Him.

May I never be separated from Him.

He is kept only by the means taught in the Gospel.

      Total and sweet renunciation.

        Etc.

Total submission to Jesus Christ and to my director.

Eternally in joy in return for a day's striving on earth.

Non obliviscar sermones tuos. [I will not forget thy words. Ps.
cxviii.16] *Amen.*

This is what I see and what troubles me. I look in all
directions and see nothing but darkness. Nature offers me
nothing that does not beget doubt and anxiety. If I saw there
nothing to indicate a Divinity, I would draw a negative con-
clusion; if I saw everywhere the marks of a Creator, I would
repose undisturbed in faith. But seeing too much to deny
and too little to assure me, I am in a pitiful state, a state in
which I have time and again wished that if Nature is sus-
tained by a God she would reveal Him unequivocally; that if
the signs which she now gives are misleading she would

suppress them altogether; that she would say all or nothing, in order that I might see which road I should follow. As it is, in my present state, ignorant of what I am and of what I ought to do, I know neither my condition nor my duty. My heart longs to know where is the true good, so that I may follow it; I could never buy eternity at too great a cost.

I envy those of the faithful whom I see living with such carelessness, who make such poor use of a gift I think I would employ so differently.

Pensées

Angelus Silesius (Johann Scheffler)
1624–1677

from The Cherubic Wanderer

The soul in whom God dwells – it is (O blest delight!)
A wandering, flowing tent of glory's endless light.

George Fox
1624–1691

Now was I come up in spirit through the flaming sword, into the paradise of God. All things were new; and all the creation gave another smell unto me than before, beyond what words can utter. I knew nothing but pureness, and innocency, and righteousness, being renewed up into the image of God by Christ Jesus, to the state of Adam, which he was in before he fell. The creation was opened to me; and it was showed me how all things had their names given them according to their nature and virtue.

Journal

A Letter to the Friends

And, Friends, though ye may have been convinced, and have tasted of the power, and felt the light; yet afterwards ye may feel a winter storm, tempest and hail, frost and cold, and temptation in the wilderness. Be patient and still in the power and in the light that doth convince you, to keep your minds to God; in that be quiet, that ye may come to the summer, that your fight be not in the winter. For if ye sit still in the patience, which overcomes in the power of God, there will be no flying.

Journal

John Bunyan
1628–1688

Now did my chains fall off from my legs indeed, I was loosed from my afflictions and irons, my temptations also fled away: so that from that time, those dreadful Scriptures of God left off to trouble me; now went I also home rejoicing, for the grace and love of God ... Now could I see myself in heaven and earth at once; in heaven by my Christ, by my head, by my righteousness and life, though on earth by my body or person.

Grace Abounding to the Chief of Sinners

... yet suddenly there fell upon me a great cloud of darkness, which did so hide from me the things of God and Christ, that I was as if I had never seen or known them in my life; I was also so overrun in my soul with a senseless heartless frame of spirit, that I could not feel my soul to move or stir after grace and life by Christ; I was as if my loins were broken, or as if my hands and feet had been tied or bound with chains . . .

After I had been in this condition some three or four days, as I was sitting by the fire, I suddenly felt this word to sound in my heart, *I must go to Jesus*; at this my former darkness and atheism fled away, and the blessed things of heaven were set within my view; while I was on this sudden thus overtaken with surprise, Wife, said I, is there ever such a scripture, *I must go to Jesus*? She said she could not tell; therefore I sat musing still to see if I could remember such a place: I had not sat above two or three minutes, but that came bolting in upon me, *And to an innumerable company of angels*, and withal, Hebrews the twelfth about the mount Zion was set before mine eyes (Heb. 12:22–4).

Then with joy I told my wife, O now I know, I know! But that night was a good night to me, I never had but few better . . . Christ was a precious Christ to my soul that night; I could scarce lie in my bed for joy, and peace, and triumph, through Christ.

Grace Abounding to the Chief of Sinners

Thomas Traherne
*c.*1634–1674

On News

News from a foreign country came,
As if my Treasure and my Wealth lay there:
So much it did my Heart Enflame!
Twas wont to call my Soul into mine Ear.
Which thither went to Meet
The Approaching Sweet:

And on the Threshold stood,
To entertain the Unknown Good.
        It Hover'd there,
        As if twould leave mine Ear,
And was so Eager to Embrace
The Joyfull Tidings as they came,
Twould almost leave its Dwelling Place,
        To Entertain the Same.

        As if the Tidings were the Things,
My very Joys themselves, my foreign Treasure,
        Or els did bear them on their Wings;
With so much Joy they came, with so much Pleasure.
        My Soul stood at the Gate
                To recreate
        Itself with Bliss: And to
        Be pleased with Speed. A fuller View
                It fain would take
                Yet Journeys back would make
Unto my Heart: as if twould fain
Go out to meet, yet stay within
To fit a place, to Entertain,
        And bring the Tidings in.

        What Sacred Instinct did inspire
My Soul in Childhood with a Hope so Strong?
        What Secret Force moved my Desire,
To expect my Joys beyond the Seas, so Yong?
        Felicity I knew
                Was out of View:
                And being here alone,
        I saw that Happiness was gone,
                From Me! for this
                I Thirsted Absent Bliss,
And thought that sure beyond the Seas,

Or els in som thing near at hand
I knew not yet, (since nought did please
   I knew.) my Bliss did stand.

   But little did the Infant Dream
That all the Treasures of the World were by:
   And that Himself was so the Cream
And Crown of all, which round about did lie.
      Yet thus it was. The Gem,
        The Diadem,
     The Ring Enclosing all
That Stood upon this Earthly Ball;
     The Heavenly Eye,
    Much Wider than the Skie,
Wherein they all included were,
The Glorious Soul that was the King
Made to possess them, did appear
    A small and little thing!

Your enjoyment of the world is never right till every morning you awake in Heaven; see yourself in your Father's
palace, and look upon the skies, the earth and the air as
celestial joys; having such a reverend esteem of all, as if you
were among the Angels. The bride of a monarch, in her
husband's chamber, hath no such causes of delight as you.

You never enjoy the world aright, till the sea itself floweth
in your veins, till you are clothed with the heavens, and
crowned with the stars: and perceive yourself to be the sole
heir of the whole world, and more than so because men are
in it who are every one sole heirs as well as you. Till you can
sing and rejoice and delight in God, as misers do in gold, and
kings in sceptres, you never enjoy the world.

Till your spirit filleth the whole world, and the stars are

your jewels; till you are as familiar with the ways of God in all ages as with your walk and table: till you are intimately acquainted with that shady nothing out of which the world was made: till you love men so as to desire their happiness, with a thirst equal to the zeal of your own: till you delight in God for being good to all: you never enjoy the world . . .

The world is a mirror of Infinite Beauty, yet no man sees it. It is a Temple of Majesty, yet no man regards it. It is a region of Light and Peace, did not men disquiet it. It is the Paradise of God. It is more to man since he is fallen than it was before. It is the place of Angels and the Gate of Heaven. When Jacob waked out of his dream, he said, God is here, and I wist it not. How dreadful is this place! This is none other than the House of God and the Gate of Heaven.

Centuries of Meditations

Charles Marshall
1637–1698

Soon I found a withdrawing again of the Lord; then I knew a winter again, and the storms of the enemy; and not having yet learned the state of being contented in want, as well as in aboundings, I not only fell into a poor, wanting, murmuring state, but also into great trouble, in a sense of this change, and fears and doubts were ready to enter: I toiled in this night, but could catch nothing which administered any comfort that was lasting . . .

Yet through the loving kindness of God, the state of resignation was opened unto me, in which man stood before he fell through transgression, into his own workings and willings. Now, when my understanding was thus opened, my soul cried out unto the Lord my God, – Oh! Preserve me in pure patience and passiveness and in living, acceptable obedience, and I will trust in thee.

And as I believed in the light of the Lord, and thereby and therein was comprehended and resigned, his pure power, love and life broke in as formerly, which greatly refreshed; then the sun shined upon my tabernacle and I bowed before the Lord, blessing and praising his holy, glorious name; then he instructed me, *and his pure Spirit and power opened in me the way of preservation, and that was, to center down into true humility.* So then my soul began to be as the dove that found a place for the soles of her feet.

> *The Journal, Together With Sundry Epistles and*
> *Other Writings of Charles Marshall*

William Penn
1644–1718

A Letter to the Countess of Falkenstein and Bruck, at Mulheim

Duysburg, the 13th of the Seventh month, 1677

And in this seeking state I was directed to the testimony of Jesus in my own conscience, as the true shining light, giving me to discern the thoughts and intents of my own heart. And no sooner was I turned unto it, but I found it to be that which from my childhood had visited me, though I distinctly knew it not. And when I received it in the love of it, it showed me all that ever I had done, and reproved all the unfruitful works of darkness, judging me as a man in the flesh, and laying judgment to the line, and righteousness to the plummet in me. And as by the brightness of his coming into my soul, He discovered the man of sin there upon his throne; so by the breath of his mouth, which is the two-edged sword of his Spirit, he destroyeth his power and kingdom. And having made me a witness of the death of the cross, He hath also made me a witness of his resurrection. So that in good measure my soul can now say I am justified in the spirit, and though the state of condemnation unto death was glorious, yet justification unto life was and is more glorious.

In this state of the new man all is new. Behold, new heavens and a new earth! Old things come to be done away; the old man with his deeds put off. Now, new thoughts, new desires, new affections, new love, new friendship, new society, new kindred, new faith, even that which overcometh this world through many tribulations; and new hope, even that living hope that is founded upon true experience, which holds out all storms, and can see to the glory that is invisible to carnal eyes, in the midst of the greatest tempest.

Journal of My Travels in Holland and Germany

Edward Taylor

*c.*1644–1729

Oh the sight of [it], oh a lost State, oh a deceitfull heart, a colde heart, a [har]d heart, a formall heart, neglect of Christ, deadness in duty, [lov]e of vanity, and the like: how did and do these Stare in my face – ... and altho' I prayed, this nei[ther] availd: but Still deadness, dulness, unspiritualness. Watch[fulne]ss would not do, heart examination oftimes ended in a [dete]station: hence an universall weriness of myselfe, disqui[et] with myselfe, judging of myselfe, Battlings of myselfe, [follo]wed, and I find with the Apostle Phil 3.8. all things of mine dung and dogs meat.

Preparatory Meditations

Cotton Mather
1663–1728

[*May 1681*] Oh! the *Hardness* of my Heart! If Mercies could
have softned or quickned mee I should not have been as I
am; but here is *desperate Wickedness*, from which I am yett
uncleansed. I have sometimes thought I should never come
to this Pass, when in secret Places, my filled Soul has been
satisfied with the communion of the blessed God. But nothing will now work in mee! Oh! I am as fitt for *Sickness*, as
ever any poor Creature was. *Fitt*, in the same Sense, that a
rotten Stump, is *fitt* for the Fire. And, *Lord*, shall I never bee
awakened, until I feel the heavy *Blowes* of thy Hand?
However, I have this to say. *First, Lord*, Thou canst *rectify* my
Spirit every Way, without such bitter *Corrections*, as I have
Reason to expect. *Next, Lord*, yett if thou will *afflict* mee, yett
if I may bee brought thereby to *see* thee more, and love thee
more, I *submitt*; here I am; afflict mee; do what thou wilt with
mee; *kill* mee; for thy *Grace* hath made mee willing to dy;
only, only, only, help mee to delight in thee, and to glorify thy
dearest Name.

Reserved Memorials

7

From Elizabeth Singer Rowe to William Wordsworth:
18th–19th century

Elizabeth Singer Rowe
1674–1737

Oh, let not the Lord be angry, and I, who am but dust, will speak. Why dost thou withdraw thyself, and suffer me to pursue thee in vain? If I am surrounded with thy immensity, why am I thus unaware of thee? Why do I not find thee, if thou art everywhere present? I seek thee in the temple, where thou hast often met me; there I have seen the traces of thy majesty and beauty; but those sacred visions bless my sight no more. I seek thee in my secret retirements, where I have called upon thy name, and have often heard the whispers of thy voice; that celestial conversation hath often reached and raptured my soul, but I am solaced no more with thy divine condescension. I listen, but I hear those gentle sounds no more. I pine and languish, but thou fleest me. Still I wither in thy absence, as a drooping plant for the reviving sun.

Devout Exercises of the Heart

William Law
1686–1761

Thou needest not, therefore, run here or there, saying 'Where is Christ?' Thou needest not say, 'Who shall ascend into heaven, that is, to bring Christ down from above? Or who shall descend into the deep, to bring Christ up from the dead?' For behold the Word, which is the Wisdom of God is in thy heart; it is there as a Bruiser of thy serpent, as a light unto thy feet, and lantern unto thy paths. It is there as an holy oil to soften and overcome the wrathful, fiery properties of thy nature, and change them into the humble meekness of light and love. It is there as a speaking Word of God in thy soul and as soon as thou art ready to hear, this eternal speaking Word will bring forth the birth of Christ, with all His holy nature, spirit and tempers, within thee; hence it was (that is, from this Principle of heaven, or Christ, in the soul), hence, I say, it was that so many eminent spirits, partakers of a divine life, have appeared in so many parts of the heathen world; glorious names, sons of wisdom, that shone, as lights hung out by God, in the midst of idolatrous darkness.

Liberal and Mystical Writings

Jonathan Edwards
1703–1758

I used to be a Person uncommonly terrified with Thunder: and it used to strike me with Terror, when I saw a Thunderstorm rising. But now, on the contrary, it rejoyced me. I felt GOD at the first Appearance of a Thunder-storm. And used to take the Opportunity, at such Times, to fix myself to view the Clouds, and see the Lightnings play, and hear the majestick and awful Voice of God's Thunder: which often times was exceeding entertaining, leading me to sweet Contemplations of my great and glorious God.

A Personal Narrative

John Wesley
1703–1791

May 1738

In the evening I went very unwillingly to a society in Aldersgate Street, where one was reading Luther's preface to the Epistle to the Romans. About a quarter before nine, while he was describing the change which God works in the heart through faith in Christ, I felt my heart strangely warmed. I felt I did trust in Christ, Christ alone, for salvation: and an Assurance was given me that he had taken away *my* sins, even *mine*, and saved *me* from the law of sin and death.

I began to pray with all my might for those who had in a more especial manner despitefully used me and persecuted me. I then testified openly to all there that what I now first felt in my heart. But it was not long before the enemy suggested, 'This cannot be faith; for where is your joy?' Then was I taught that peace and victory over sin are essential to faith in the captain of our salvation; but that, as to the transports of joy that usually attend the beginning of it, especially in those who have mourned deeply, God sometimes gives, sometimes withholds them, according to the counsels of his own will.

After my return home, I was much buffeted with temptations; but I cried out, and they fled away. They returned again and again. I as often lifted up my eyes, and he 'sent me help from his holy place'. And I found the difference between this and my former state chiefly consisted in this. I was striving, yes, fighting with all my might under the law, as well as under grace. But then I was sometimes, if not often, conquered; now, I was always conquered.

Thursday 25. The moment I awoke, 'Jesus, master' was in my heart and in my mouth; and I found all my strength lay in keeping my eye fixed on him, and my soul waiting on him continually.

The Journal of the Rev. John Wesley

The Tree of Life
18th(?) century

The tree of life my soul hath seen
Laden with fruit and always green:
The trees of nature fruitless be
Compared with Christ the apple tree.

His beauty doth all things excel:
By faith I know, but ne'er can tell
The glory which I now can see
In Jesus Christ the apple tree.

For happiness I long have sought,
And pleasure dearly I have bought:
I missed of all, but now I see
'Tis found in Christ the apple tree.

I'm weary with my former toil,
Here I will sit and rest awhile:
Under the shadow I will be
Of Jesus Christ the apple tree.

This fruit doth make my soul to thrive,
It keeps my dying faith alive,
Which makes my soul in haste to be
With Jesus Christ the apple tree.

Anon

Charles Wesley
1707–1788

Wrestling Jacob

Come, O thou Traveller unknown
   Whom still I hold, but cannot see,
My company before is gone,
   And I am left alone with thee,
With thee all night I mean to stay,
And wrestle till the break of day.

I need not tell thee who I am,
   My misery and sin declare,
Thyself hast called me by my name,
   Look on thy hands, and read it there,
But who, I ask thee, who art thou?
Tell me thy name, and tell me now.

In vain thou strugglest to get free,
   I never will unloose my hold:
Art thou the Man that died for me?
   The secret of thy love unfold.
Wrestling, I will not let thee go,
Till I thy name, thy nature know.

   . . .

Yield to me now – for I am weak;
   But confident in self-despair:
Speak to my heart, in blessings speak,
   Be conquered by my instant prayer,
Speak, or thou never hence shalt move,
And tell me, if thy name is Love.

'Tis Love, 'tis Love! Thou died'st for me,
   I hear thy whisper in my heart.
The morning breaks, the shadows flee:
   Pure Universal Love thou art;
To me, to all, thy bowels move,
Thy nature and thy name is Love.

My prayer hath power with God; the Grace
   Unspeakable I now receive,
Through Faith I see thee face to face,
   I see thee face to face, and live:
In vain I have not wept, and strove,
Thy nature and thy name is Love.

I know thee, Saviour, who thou art,
   Jesus, the feeble sinner's friend;
Nor wilt thou with the night depart,
   But stay, and love me to the end;
Thy mercies never shall remove,
Thy nature and thy name is Love.

The Sun of Righteousness on me
   Hath rose with healing in His wings.
Withered my nature's strength; from thee
   My soul its life and succour brings,
My help is all laid up above;
Thy nature and thy name is Love.

Contented now upon thy thigh
   I halt, till life's short journey end;
All helplessness, all weakness I
   On thee alone for strength depend,
Nor have I power from thee to move;
Thy nature and thy name is Love.

Lame as I am, I take the prey,
    Hell, earth and sin with ease o'ercome;
I leap for joy, pursue my way,
    And as a bounding hart fly home,
Through all eternity to prove
Thy nature and thy name is Love.

Samuel Johnson
1709–1784

Dr Johnson talks to Dr Adams, master of Pembroke College, Oxford, where Johnson had studied:

JOHNSON. .... as I cannot be sure that I have fulfilled the conditions on which salvation is granted, I am afraid I may be one of those who shall be damned.' (looking dismally.) DR ADAMS. 'What do you mean by damned?' JOHNSON. (passionately and loudly) 'Sent to Hell, Sir, and punished everlastingly.'... BOSWELL. 'But may not a man attain to such a degree of hope as not to be uneasy from the fear of death?' JOHNSON. 'A man may have such a degree of hope as to keep him quiet. You see I am not quiet, from the vehemence with which I talk; but I do not despair.'

Life of Samuel Johnson

Nathan Cole
1711–1783

I believe I felt just as the Apostles felt the truth of the word when they writ it, every leaf line and letter smiled in my face; I got the bible up under my Chin and hugged it ... Now my heart talked with God; now every thing that was sin fled from the presence of God: as far as darkness is gone from light or beams of the sun for where ever the Sun can be seen clear there is no darkness.

Spiritual Travels

Laurence Sterne
1713–1768

Sermon on the Prodigal Son

... And he said unto his servants, Bring forth the best robe and put it on him; and put a ring on his hand and shoes on his feet, and bring hither the fatted calf, and let us eat and drink and be merry

When the affections so kindly break loose, Joy is another name for Religion.

We look up as we taste it: the cold Stoic without, when he hears the dancing and the music, may ask sullenly, (with the elder brother) What it means? And refuse to enter: but the humane and compassionate all fly impetuously to the banquet, given for a son who was dead and is alive again, – who was lost and is found. Gentle spirits, light up the pavilion with a sacred fire; and parental love, and filial piety lead in the mask with riot and wild festivity! Was it not for this that GOD gave man music to strike upon the kindly passions; that nature taught the feet to dance to its movements, and as chief governess of the feast poured forth wine into the goblet, to crown it with gladness?

Howell Harris
1714–1773

June 18th 1735: being in secret prayer, I felt suddenly my heart melting within me like wax before the fire with love of God my saviour; and felt not only love, peace etc, but longing to be dissolved, and to be with Christ. Then was a cry in my inmost soul, which I was totally unacquainted with before, Abba Father! Abba, Father! I could not help calling God my Father; I knew that I was His child, and that he loved me and heard me. My soul being filled and satiated, crying, 'Tis enough, I am satisfied. Give me strength, and I will follow Thee through fire and water.' I could say I was happy indeed. There was in me a well of water springing up to everlasting life, John 4:14. The love of God was shed abroad in my heart by the Holy Ghost.

Journals

John Woolman
1720–1772

26/8/1772

In a time of Sickness with the plurisie, a little upward of two years and a half ago I was brought so Near the gates of death, that I forgot my name. Being then desirous to know who I was, I saw a mass of matter of a dull gloomy collour, between the South and the East, and was informed that this mass was human beings, in as great misery as they could be, & live, and that I was mixed in with them, & henceforth I might not consider myself as a distinct or Separate being. In this state I remained several hours. I then heard a soft melodious voice, more pure and harmonious than any voice I had heard with my ears before, and I believed it was the voice of an angel who spake to the other angels. The words were *John Woolman is dead.* I soon remembered that I once was John Woolman, and being assured that I was alive in the body, I greatly wondered what that heavenly voice could mean.

I believed beyond doubting that it was the voice of an holy Angel, but as yet it was a mystery to me …

My tongue was often so dry that I could not speak till I had moved it about and gathered some moisture, and as I lay still for a time, at length I felt divine power prepare my mouth that I could speak, and then I said, 'I am crucified with Christ, nevertheless I live yet not I, but Christ [that] liveth in me, and the life I now live in the flesh is by faith [in] the Son of God who loved me and gave himself for me.'

Then the Mystery was opened and I perceived there was Joy in heaven over a Sinner who had repented, and that that language, *John Woolman is dead*, meant no more than the death of my own will.

The Journal of the Voyage

Friedrich Gottlieb Klopstock
1724–1803

Wissbegierde (Desire for Knowledge)

The sun went down, twilight came; the moon rose, Hesperus shone and inspired me. Oh, how pregnant with meaning were the words of God – for it was He who was speaking – which my eye saw!

The light faded, Thunderclaps rumbled, the storm and the roaring of the sea were beautiful and awe-inspiring and exalted my heart. Oh, how pregnant with meaning were the words of God – for it was He who was speaking – which I heard sounding!

God rules, beckoning, directing, as beings act who are free; He rules the present and the future. Does God speak, too, through the deeds mortals do? If this is so (and who does not glow with restless thirst to know?) what does He reveal through the triumphs of those who deny not only human rights but even God Himself?

As I wander on the shores of the ocean, on which we shall all of us drift at last, I shall soon discover it. I want to quench my burning desire for knowledge. It remains, it is a holy fire!

They sow a seed, the harvest of which is desolation. They deny human rights and deny God. Does not God now keep silence withholding His guidance? And can you alone, terrible silence, save us?

William Cowper
1731–1800

'The Lord will Happiness divine'

The Lord will happiness divine
   On contrite hearts bestow;
Then tell me, gracious God, is mine
   A contrite heart, or no?

I hear, but seem to hear in vain,
   Insensible as steel;
If aught is felt, 'tis only pain
   To find I cannot feel.

I sometimes think myself inclined
   To love Thee, if I could;
But often feel another mind,
   Averse to all that's good.

My best desires are faint and few,
   I fain would strive for more;
But when I cry, 'My strength renew',
   Seem weaker than before.

Thy saints are comforted, I know,
   And love Thy house of prayer;
I therefore go where others go,
   But find no comfort there.

Oh make this heart rejoice, or ache;
   Decide this doubt for me;
And if it be not broken, break,
   And heal it, if it be.

Walking with God

Oh! for a closer walk with God,
   A calm and heavenly frame;
A light to shine upon the road
   That leads me to the Lamb!

Where is the blessedness I knew
   When first I saw the Lord?
Where is the soul-refreshing view
   Of Jesus and his word?

What peaceful hours I once enjoyed!
   How sweet their memory still!
But they have left an aching void
   The world can never fill.

Return, O holy Dove, return,
   Sweet messenger of rest;
I hate sins that made thee mourn,
   And drove thee from my breast.

The dearest idol I have known,
   Whate'er that idol be;
Help me to tear it from thy throne,
   And worship only Thee.

So shall my walk be close with God,
   Calm and serene my frame;
So purer light shall mark the road
   That leads me to the Lamb.

James Boswell
1740–1795

Boswell visits the dying David Hume, famous sceptic philosopher.

3 March 1777

I asked him if he was not religious when he was young. He said he was ... He then said flatly that the morality of every religion was bad, and, I really thought, he was not jocular when he said that when he heard a man was religious, he concluded he was a rascal, though he had known some instances of very good men being religious ...

I had a strong curiosity to be satisfied if he persisted in disbelieving a future state even when he had death before his eyes. I was persuaded from what he now said, and from his manner of saying it, that he did persist. I asked him if it was not possible that there might be a future state. He answered it was possible that a piece of coal put upon the fire would not burn; and he added that it was a most unreasonable fancy that we should exist forever ...

I asked him if the thought of annihilation never gave him any uneasiness. He said not the least ... I however felt a degree of horror, mixed with a sort of wild, strange, hurrying recollection of my excellent mother's pious instructions, of Dr Johnson's noble lessons, and of my religious sentiments and affections during the course of my life. I was like a man in sudden danger eagerly seeking his defensive arms; and I could not but be assailed by momentary doubts while I had actually before me a man of such strong abilities and extensive inquiry dying in the persuasion of being annihilated. But I maintained my faith.

An Account of my Last Interview with David Hume Esq

Johann Wolfgang von Goethe
1749–1832

Faust's Confession

I, image of the Godhead, who deemed myself but now
On the brink of the mirror of eternal truth and seeing
My rapturous fill of the blaze of clearest Heaven,
Having stripped off my earthly being;
I, more than an angel, I whose boundless urge
To flow through Nature's veins and in the act of creation
To revel it like the gods – what a divination,
What an act of daring – and what an expiation!
One thundering word has swept me over the verge.

To boast myself thine equal I do not dare.
Granted I owned the power to draw thee down,
I lacked the power to hold thee there.
In that blest moment I felt myself,
Felt myself so small, so great;
Cruelly thou didst thrust me back
Into man's uncertain fate.
Who will teach me? What must I shun?

Or must I go where that impulse drives?
Alas, our very actions like our sufferings
Put a brake upon our lives.

Goethe's Faust
translated by Louis MacNeice

William Blake

1757–1827

from Jerusalem

Awake! Awake O sleeper of the land of shadows, wake!
expand!

I am in you and you in me, mutual in love divine:
Fibres of love from man to man thro Albion's pleasant land.
In all the dark Atlantic vale down from the hills of Surrey
A black water accumulates; return Albion! return!
Thy brethren call thee, and thy fathers and thy sons,
Thy nurses and thy mothers, thy sisters and thy daughters
Weep at thy soul's disease, and the Divine Vision is darkened:
Thy Emanation that was wont to play before thy face,
Beaming forth with her daughters into the Divine bosom:
Where hast thou hidden thy Emanation, lovely Jerusalem,
From the vision and fruition of the Holy-one?
I am not a God afar off, I am a brother and friend:
Within your bosoms I reside, and you reside in me:
Lo! We are One; forgiving all Evil; Not seeking recompense!
Ye are my members, O ye sleepers of Beulah, land of shades!

William Wordsworth
1770–1850

from The Excursion

Far and wide the clouds were touch'd,
And in their silent faces could he read
Unutterable love. Sound needed none,
Nor any voice of joy; his spirit drank
The spectacle: sensation, soul, and form,
All melted into him; they swallow'd up
His animal being; in them did he live,
And by them did he live; they were his life.
In such access of mind, in such high hour
Of visitation from the living God,
Thought was not; in enjoyment it expir'd.
No thanks he breath'd; he proffer'd no request;
Rapt into still communion that transcends
The imperfect offices of prayer and praise,
His mind was a thanksgiving to the power
That made him; it was blessedness and love!

From Zilpha Elaw to Henry Handel Richardson:
19th–20th century

Zilpha Elaw
c.1780–1846

1836

And while I was thus engaged, it seemed as if I heard my God rustling in the tops of the mulberry trees. Oh, how precious was this day to my soul!

Memoirs of the Life, Religious Experience, Ministerial Travels and Labours of Mrs Zilpha Elaw, An American Female of Color; Together with Some Accounts of the Great Religious Revivals in America [Written by Herself]

St John Vianney, Curé d'Ars
1786–1869

There was a simple peasant, a good father of a family, an unlettered husbandman, whose fervent piety was the joy of his pastor's heart. Whether going to his work or returning from it, never did that good man pass the church door without entering it to adore his Lord. He would leave his tools, his spade, hoe, and pickaxe, at the door and remain for hours together sitting or kneeling before the tabernacle. M. Vianney, who watched him with great delight, could never perceive the slightest movement of the lips. Being surprised at this circumstance, he said to him one day, 'My good father, what do you say to our Lord in these long visits you pay him every day and many times a day?' 'I say nothing to him,' was the reply; 'I look at him, and he looks at me.' 'A beautiful and sublime answer,' says M. Monnin. He said nothing, he opened no book, he could not read; but he had eyes – eyes of the body and eyes of the soul – and he opened them, those of the soul especially, and fixed them on our Lord. 'I look at him.' He fastened upon him his whole mind, his whole heart; all his sense, and all his faculties. There was an interchange of ineffable thought in those glances which came and went between the heart of the servant and the heart of the Master. This is the secret, the great secret, of attaining sanctity.

Life of the Blessed Curé D'Ars

Augustus William Hare
1792–1834

That ball of heat and light, which we call most properly the Sun, may be compared to the Father, from whom both the Word and the Spirit come. From this sun the light issues, and is as it were a part of it, and yet comes down to our earth, and gives light to us. This we may compare to the Word, who came forth from the Father, and came down to earth and was made man and who, as St John tells us, is 'the true light, which lighteth every man that cometh into the world.' But beside this there is the heat, which is a different thing from the light: for all we know, there may be heat without light: and so may there be light, – moonlight for example and starlight, – without any perceivable heat. Yet the two are blended and united in the sun; so that the same rays, which bring us light to enlighten us, bring us heat also to warm us, and to ripen the fruits and herbs of all kinds which the earth bears. This heat of the sun may not unfitly be compared to the Holy Spirit, the Lord and Giver of life, as the Creed calls him, for heat is the great fosterer of life: as we see for example in an egg. As that is hatched by the warmth of the parent bird, sitting on it lovingly, and brooding over it, until it is quickened into life; just so does the Holy Spirit of God brood with more than dove-like patience over the heart of the believer, giving it life and warmth; and though he be driven away again and again by our backslidings, he still hovers round our hearts, desiring to return to them, and to dwell in them, and cherish them for ever. Moreover, if any seed of the Word has begun to spring up in any heart, the Spirit descends like a sunbeam upon it, and ripens the ear, and brings the fruit to perfection. Thus have we first the sun in the sky, secondly the light which issues from the sun, and thirdly, the heat, which accompanies the light, – three separate and distinguishable things; yet distinct as they are, what can be more united than the sun and its rays, or than the light and heat which those rays shed abroad?

Holy Branches: Why was the Trinity Revealed?

Sojourner Truth
c.1797–1883

She talked to God as familiarly as if he had been a creature like herself; and a thousand times more so, than if she had been in the presence of some earthly potentate. She demanded, with little expenditure of reverence or fear, a supply of all her more pressing wants, and at times her demands approached very near to commands. She felt as if

God was under obligation to her, much more than she was to him. He seemed to her benighted vision in some manner bound to do her bidding.

Her heart recoils now, with very dread, when she recalls those shocking, almost blasphemous conversations with the great Jehovah. And well for herself did she deem it, that, unlike earthly potentates, his infinite character combined the tender father with the omniscient and omnipotent Creator of the universe.

The Narrative of Sojourner Truth

John Henry Newman
1801–1890

Sunday June 13 1824 (2 days after his ordination)
It is over. I am thine, O Lord. I feel quite dizzy, and cannot altogether believe and understand it. At first after the hands were laid upon me, my heart shuddered within me – the words 'for ever' are so terrible. It was hardly a godly feeling which made me feel melancholy at the idea of giving it all up for God. At times indeed my heart burnt within me, particularly during the singing of the Veni Creator. Yet, Lord, I do not ask for comfort in comparison of sanctification. O! I feel as a man thrown suddenly in deep water.

Diaries

The Pillar of the Cloud

Lead, kindly light, amid the encircling gloom,
    Lead thou me on:
The night is dark, and I am far from home;
    Lead thou me on.

Keep thou my feet; I do not ask to see
The distant scene: one step enough for me.

I was not ever thus, nor prayed that thou
    Shouldst lead me on;
I loved to choose and see my path; but now
    Lead thou me on.
I loved the garish day, and, spite of fears,
Pride ruled my will: remember not past years.

So long the power hath blest me, sure it still
    Will lead me on
O'er moor and fen, o'er crag and torrent, till
    The night is gone,
And with the morn those angel faces smile
Which I have loved long since, and lost awhile.

Ralph Waldo Emerson
1803–1882

Standing on the bare ground, my head bathed by the blithe air, and uplifted into infinite space – all mean egotism vanishes. I become a transparent eyeball. I am nothing. I see all. The currents of the Universal Being circulate through me. I am part or [a] particle of God.

Journals and Miscellaneous Notebooks

Alfred, Lord Tennyson
1809–1892
from In Memoriam

That which we dare invoke to bless;
    Our dearest faith; our ghastliest doubt;
    He, They, One, All; within, without;
The Power in darkness Whom we guess.

I found Him not in world or sun,
 Or eagle's wing, or insect's eye;
 Nor through the questions men may try,
The petty cobwebs we have spun.

If e'er when faith had fallen asleep,
 I heard a voice 'Believe no more',
 And heard an ever-breaking shore
That tumbled in the Godless deep;

A warmth within the breast would melt
 The freezing reason's colder part,
 And like a man in wrath the heart
Stood up and answer'd 'I have felt'.

No, like a child in doubt and fear:
 But that blind clamour made me wise;
 Then was I as a child that cries,
But, crying, knows his father near;

And what I seem beheld again
 What is, and no man understands;
 And out of darkness came the hands
That reach through nature, moulding men.

Søren Kierkegaard
1813–1855

1838
May 19 Half-past ten in the morning. There is an indescribable joy which enkindles us as inexplicably as the apostle's outburst comes gratuitously: 'Rejoice I say unto you, and again I say unto you rejoice'. – Not a joy over this or that but the

soul's mighty song 'with tongue and mouth, from the bottom of the heart': 'I rejoice through my joy, in, at, with, over, by, and with my joy' – a heavenly refrain, as it were, suddenly breaks off our other song; a joy which cools and refreshes us like a breath of wind, a wave of air, from the trade wind which blows from the plains of Mamre to the everlasting habitations.

The Journals of Søren Kierkegaard

1849

In suffering and tribulation there are really certain situations in which, humanly speaking, the thought of God and that he is nevertheless love, makes the suffering far more exhausting. In such cases faith is being tried and love put to the test, to see whether one really loves God, really cannot do without him. Humanly speaking one who suffered and was tried thus would be justified in saying: it would all be less painful to me if I did not at the same time have the idea of God. For either one suffers at the thought that God the all-powerful, who could so easily help, leaves one helpless, or else one suffers because one's reason is crucified by the thought that God is love all the same and that what happens to one is for one's good. Humanly speaking it is terrible only to have an opinion and a scrap of understanding about that which one should, so it would seem, be able to judge: one's own suffering – to be even less than a sparrow. Despair makes everything easier because it is an undisturbed agreement with oneself that the suffering is unbearable. The further effort which the idea of God demands of us is to have to understand that suffering must not only be borne but that it is a good, a gift of the God of love ...

Yet this is only a tribulation, which may be terrible enough as long as it lasts. But it is blessed to endure with

God. In the first case the only thing is to call immediately upon one's idea of God, and that brings relief. In the second case (and this is the real tribulation) it seems that the idea of God itself increases the suffering. Then one must continue to endure it in faith. If you do not lose hold of God you will ultimately find blessed agreement with God that the suffering was kindness. For God wishes to be right, unconditionally; oh, but the highest blessedness is to put God in the right precisely when, humanly speaking, there seems almost to be an objection to be brought against him. God wishes to be believed, unconditionally; but one who is infinite cannot but put the price of faith infinitely high. Oh, but it is blessed to believe, and the higher the price the greater the happiness; the dearer you buy, the happier you will be.

The Journals of Søren Kierkegaard

1849

Sep 28. What is true of the relation between two men is not true of the relation of man to God: that the longer they live together and the better they get to know each other the closer do they come to one another. The opposite is true in relation to God; the longer one lives with him the more infinite he becomes, – and the smaller one becomes oneself. Alas, as a child it seemed as though God and man could play together. Alas, in youth one dreamed that if one really tried with all the passion of a man in love, though adoring at the same time, the relationship might yet be brought into being. Alas, as a man one discovers how infinite God is and the infinite distance.

The Journals of Søren Kierkegaard

Emily Brontë
1818–1848

The Prisoner

'Still let my tyrants know, I am not doomed to wear
Year after year in gloom, and desolate despair;
A messenger of Hope comes every night to me,
And offers for short life, eternal liberty.

'He comes with western winds, with evening's wandering
   airs,
With that clear dusk of heaven that brings the thickest stars,
Winds take a pensive tone, and stars a tender fire,
And visions rise, and change, that kill me with desire.

'Desire for nothing known in my maturer years,
When Joy grew mad with awe, at counting future tears.
When, if my spirit's sky was full of flashes warm,
I knew not whence they came, from sun or thunder-storm.

'But first, a hush of peace – a soundless calm descends;
The struggle of distress, and fierce impatience ends;
Mute music soothes my breast – unuttered harmony,
That I could never dream, till Earth was lost to me.

'Then dawns the Invisible; the Unseen its truth reveals;
My outward sense is gone, my inward essence feels:
Its wings are almost free – its home, its harbour found,
Measuring the gulf, it stoops and dares the final bound.

'O! dreadful is the check – intense the agony –
When the ear begins to hear, and the eye begins to see;
When the pulse begins to throb, the brain to think again;
The soul to feel the flesh, and the flesh to feel the chain.

'Yet I would lose no sting, would wish no torture less;
The more that anguish racks, the earlier it will bless;
And robed in fires of hell, or bright with heavenly shine,
If it but herald death, the vision is divine!'

Walt Whitman
1819–1892

from The Prayer of Columbus

One effort more, my altar this bleak sand:
That Thou, O God, my life has lighted,
With ray of light, steady, ineffable, vouchsafed of Thee,
Light rare untellable, lighting the very light,
Beyond all signs, descriptions, languages;
For that, O God, be it my latest word, here on my knees,
Old, poor, and paralysed, I thank Thee.

My terminus near,
The clouds already closing in upon me,
The voyage balk'd, the course disputed, lost,
I yield my ships to Thee.

John Ruskin
1819–1900

Letter to Henry Acland after having read
Sir Charles Lyell's *Principles of Geology*

You speak of the flimsiness of your own faith. Mine, which
was never strong, is being beaten into mere gold leaf, and
flutters in weak rags from the letter of its old forms; but the
only letters it can hold by at all are the old Evangelical
formulae. If only the Geologists would let me alone, I could

do very well, but those dreadful Hammers! I hear the clink
of them at the end of every cadence of the Bible verses.

George MacDonald
1824–1905

from The Diary of an Old Soul

January

Sometimes, hard trying, it seems I cannot pray –
For doubt, and pain, and anger, and all strife.
Yet some poor half-fledged prayer-bird from the nest
May fall, flit, perch – crouch in the bowery breast
Of the large nation-healing tree of life; –
Moveless there sit through all the burning day,
And on my heart at night a fresh leaf cooling lay.

My harvest withers. Health, my means to live –
All things seem rushing straight into the dark.
But the dark still is God. I would not give
The smallest silver-piece to turn the rush
Backward or sideways. Am I not a spark
Of him who is the light? – Fair hope doth flush
My east. – Divine success – Oh, hush and hark!

Thy will be done. I yield up everything.
'The life is more than meat' – then more than health;
'The body is more than raiment' – more than wealth;
The hairs I made not, thou art numbering.
Thou art my life – I the brook, thou the spring.
Because thine eyes are open, I can see;
Because thou art thyself, 'tis there I am me.

October

From sleep I wake, and wake to think of thee.
But wherefore not with sudden glorious glee?
Why burst not gracious on me heaven and earth
In all the splendour of a new-day birth?
Why hangs a cloud between my lord and me?
The moment that my eyes the morning greet,
My soul should panting rush to clasp God's feet.

Is it because it is not thou I see,
But only my poor blotted fancy of thee?
Oh! Never till thyself reveal thy face,
Shall I be flooded with life's vital grace!
Oh make my mirror-heart thy shining-place,
And then my soul, awaking with the morn,
Shall be a waking joy, eternally new-born.

Leo Tolstoy
1828–1910

But again and again and from various directions I kept
coming back to the conviction that I could not have come
into the world without any motive, cause, or meaning, that I
could not be the fledgling fallen from a nest that I felt myself
to be. If I lie on my back in the tall grass and cry out like a
fallen fledgling, it is because my mother brought me into the
world, kept me warm, fed me, and loved me. But where is
my mother now? If I have been cast out, then who has cast
me out? I cannot help but feel that someone who loved me
gave birth to me. Who is this someone? Again, God.

Confession

At the age of twenty-six, while taking shelter for the night during a hunting trip, he knelt to pray in the evening, as had been his custom since his childhood. His older brother, who had accompanied him on the trip, was lying down on some straw and watching him. When S. had finished and was getting ready to lie down, his brother said to him, 'So you still do that.' And they said nothing more to each other. From that day S. gave up praying and going to church. And for thirty years he has not prayed, he has not taken communion, and he has not gone to church. Not because he shared his brother's convictions and went along with them; nor was it because he had decided on something or other in his own soul. It was simply that the remark his brother had made was like the nudge of a finger against a wall that was about to fall over from its own weight. His brother's remark showed him that the place where he thought faith to be had long since been empty; subsequently the words he spoke, the signs of the cross he made, and the bowing of his head in prayer were in essence completely meaningless actions. Once having admitted the meaninglessness of these gestures, he could no longer continue them.

Confession

Five years ago I came to believe in Christ's teaching and my life suddenly changed ... It happened to me as it happens to a man who goes out on some business and on the way suddenly decides that the business is unnecessary and returns home. All that was on his right is now on his left and all that was on his left is now on his right; his former wish to get as far as possible from home has changed into a wish to be as near as possible to it. The direction of my life and my desires became different, and good and evil changed places ...

I, like the thief on the cross, have believed Christ's teaching and been saved . . . I, like the thief, knew that I was unhappy and suffering . . . I, like the thief to the cross was nailed by some force to that life of suffering and evil. And as, after the meaningless suffering and evils of life, the thief awaited the terrible darkness of death, so did I await the same thing.

In all this I was exactly like the thief, but the difference was that the thief was already dying while I was still living. The thief might believe that his salvation lay there beyond the grave but I could not be satisfied with that, because, besides a life beyond the grave, life still awaited me here. But I did not understand that life. It seemed to me terrible. And suddenly I heard the words of Christ and understood them, and life and death ceased to seem to me evil, and instead of despair I experienced happiness and the joy of life undisturbed by death.

What I Believe

Emily Dickinson
1830–1886

A loss of something ever felt I

A loss of something ever felt I –
The first that I could recollect
Bereft I was – of what I knew not
Too young that any should suspect
A Mourner walked among the children
I notwithstanding went about
As one bemoaning a Dominion
Itself the only Prince cast out –
Elder, Today, a session wiser
And fainter, too, as Wiseness is –
I find myself still softly searching
For my Delinquent Palaces –

And a Suspicion, like a Finger
Touches my Forehead now and then
That I am looking oppositely
For the site of the Kingdom of Heaven –

He fumbles at your soul

He fumbles at your Soul
As Players at the Keys
Before they drop full Music on –
He stuns you by degrees –
Prepares your brittle Nature
For the Ethereal Blow
By fainter Hammers – further heard –
Then nearer – then so slow
Your breath has time to straighten –
Your Brain – to bubble Cool –
Deals – One – Imperial – Thunderbolt –
That scalps your naked Soul –

When Winds take Forests in their Paws –
The Universe – is still –

Christina Rossetti
1830–1894

from Despised and Rejected

'Then I cried out upon him: Cease,
Leave me in peace;
Fear not that I should crave
Aught thou mayst have.
Leave me in peace, yea trouble me no more,
Lest I arise and chase thee from my door.

What, shall I not be let
Alone, that thou dost vex me yet?

But all night long that voice spake urgently:
"Open to Me."
Still harping in mine ears:
"Rise, let Me in."
Pleading with tears:
"Open to Me, that I may come to thee."
While the dew dropped, while the dark hours were cold:
"My Feet bleed, see My Face,
See My Hands bleed that bring thee grace,
My Heart doth bleed for thee,
Open to Me."

So till the break of day:
Then died away
That voice, in silence as of sorrow;
Then footsteps echoing like a sigh
Passed me by,
Lingering footsteps slow to pass.
On the morrow
I saw upon the grass
Each footprint marked in blood, and on my door
The mark of blood for evermore.'

James Thomson
1834–1882

Once in a saintly passion
I cried with desperate grief,
O Lord, my heart is black with guile,
Of sinners I am chief.

Then stooped my guardian angel
And whispered from behind,
'Vanity, my little man,
You're nothing of the kind.'

Frederick Myers
1843–1901

Myers describes walking with George Eliot in the Fellows' Garden of Trinity College, Cambridge, on a rainy evening.

She, stirred somewhat beyond her wont, and taking as her text the three words which have been used so often as the trumpet-calls of men – the words, *God, Immortality, Duty* – pronounced, with terrible earnestness, how inconceivable was the *first*, how unbelievable the *second*, and yet how peremptory and absolute the *third*. Never, perhaps, have sterner accents affirmed the sovereignty of impersonal and unrecompensing law. I listened, and night fell; her grave, majestic countenance turned toward me like a sibyl's in the gloom; it was as though she withdrew from my grasp, one by one, the two scrolls of promise, and left me the third scroll only, awful with inevitable fates. And when we stood at length and parted, amid the columnar circuit of the forest-trees, beneath the last twilight of starless skies, I seemed to be gazing, like Titus at Jerusalem, on vacant seats and empty halls – on a sanctuary with no Presence to hallow it, and heaven left lonely of a God.

The Century Magazine

Gerard Manley Hopkins
1844–1889

I Wake and Feel the Fell of Dark

I wake and feel the fell of dark, not day.
What hours, O what black hours we have spent
This night! What sights you, heart, saw; ways you went!
And more must, in yet longer light's delay.
With witness I speak this. But where I say
Hours I mean years, mean life. And my lament
Is cries countless, cries like dead letters sent
To dearest him that lives alas! away.

I am gall, I am heartburn. God's most deep decree
Bitter would have me taste: my taste was me;
Bones built in me, flesh filled, blood brimmed the curse.
Selfyeast of spirit a dull dough sours. I see
The lost are like this, and their scourge to be
As I am mine, their sweating selves; but worse.

Friedrich Nietzsche
1844–1900

Have you not heard of that madman who lit a lantern in
the bright morning hours, ran to the market place, and
cried incessantly: 'I seek God! I seek God!' ... 'Whither is
God?' he cried; I will tell you. *We have killed him* – you and
I. All of us are his murderers. But how did we do this? ...
Who gave us the sponge to wipe away the entire
horizon?

The Gay Science

Richard Jefferies
1848–1887

The bright morning sun of summer heated the eastern parapet of London Bridge; I stayed in the recess to acknowledge it. The smooth water was a broad sheen of light, the built-up river flowed calm and silent by a thousand doors, rippling only where the stream chafed against a chain. Red pennants drooped, gilded vanes gleamed on polished masts, black-pitched hulls glistened like a black rook's feathers in sunlight; the clear air cut out the forward angles of the warehouses, the shadowed wharves were quiet in shadows that carried light; far down the ships that were hauling out moved in repose, and with the stream floated away into the summer mist. There was a faint blue colour in the air hovering between the built-up banks, against the lit walls, in the hollows of the houses. The swallows wheeled and climbed, twittered and glided downwards. Burning on, the great sun stood in the sky, heating the parapet. Glowing steadily upon me as when I rested in the narrow valley grooved out in prehistoric times. Burning on steadfast, and ever present as my thought. Lighting the broad river, the broad walls; lighting the least speck of dust; lighting the great heaven; gleaming on my finger-nail. The fixed point of day – the sun. I was intensely conscious of it; I felt it; I felt the presence of the immense powers of the universe; I felt out into the depths of the ether. So intensely conscious of the sun, the sky, the limitless space, I felt too in the midst of eternity then, in the midst of the supernatural, among the immortal and the greatness of the material, realised the spirit. By these I saw my soul; by these I knew the supernatural to be more intensely real than the sun. I touched the supernatural, the immortal, there that moment.

The Story of My Heart

Mrs Humphrey (Mary Augusta) Ward
1851–1920

The September wind blew about him as he strolled through the darkening common, set thick with great bushes of sombre juniper among the yellowing fern, which stretched away on the left-hand side of the road leading to the Hall. He stood and watched the masses of restless discordant cloud which the sunset had left behind it thinking the while of Mr Grey, of his assertions and his denials. Certain phrases of his, which Robert had heard drop from him on one or two rare occasions during the later stages of his Oxford life, ran through his head.

'*The fairy tale of Christianity*', '*The origins of Christian mythology*'. He could recall, as the words rose in his memory, the simplicity of the rugged face, and the melancholy mingled with fire which had always marked the great tutor's sayings about religion.

'*Fairy tale!*' Could any reasonable man watch a life like Catherine's [his wife] and believe that nothing but a delusion lay at the heart of it? And as he asked that question, he seemed to hear Mr Grey's answer: 'All religions are true, and all are false. In them all, more or less visibly, man grasps at the one thing needful – self forsaken, God laid hold of. The spirit in them all is the same, answers eternally to reality; it is but the letter, the fashion, the imagery, that are relative and changing.'

He turned and walked homeward, struggling with a host of tempestuous ideas as swift and varying as the autumn clouds hurrying overhead. And then, through a break in a line of trees, he caught sight of the tower and chancel window of the little church. In an instant he had a vision of early summer mornings – dewy, perfumed, silent, save for the birds, and all the soft stir of rural birth and growth, of a chancel fragrant with many flowers, of the kneeling form of his wife close beside him, himself bending over her, the sacrament of the Lord's death in his hand. The emotion, the intensity, the absolute self-surrender of innumerable such moments in the past – moments of a common faith, a common self-abasement – came flooding back upon him. With a movement of joy and penitence he threw himself at the feet of Catherine's Master and his own: '*fix there thy resting place my soul*'.

Robert Elsmere

Francis Thompson
1859–1907

from The Hound of Heaven

I fled Him, down the nights and down the days;
I fled Him down the arches of the years;
I fled Him down the labyrinthine ways
    Of my own mind: and in the midst of tears
I hid from Him, and under running laughter.
    Up vistaed hopes I sped;
    And shot, precipitated,
    Adown Titanic glooms of chasmed fears,
    From those strong feet that followed, followed after.
    And with unhurrying chase
    And unperturbed pace,
Deliberate speed, majestic instancy,
    They beat – and a Voice beat
    More instant than the Feet –
    'All things betray thee, who betrayest Me'
    . . .

Now of that long pursuit
Comes on at hand the bruit;
That voice is round me like a bursting sea:
'And is thy earth so marred,
Shattered in shard on shard?
Lo, all things fly thee, for thou fliest Me!
Strange, piteous, futile thing!
Wherefore should any set thee love apart?
Seeing none but I makes much of naught' (He said),
'And human love needs human meriting:
How hast thou merited –
Of all man's clotted clay the dingiest clot?
Alack, thou knowest not
How little worthy of any love thou art!
Whom wilt thou find to love ignoble thee,
Save Me, save only Me?
All which I took from thee I did but take,
Not for thy harms,
But just that thou might'st seek it in My arms.
All which thy child's mistake
Fancies as lost, I have stored for thee at home:
Rise, clasp My hand, and come!'

Halts by me that footfall:
Is my gloom, after all,
Shade of His hand, outstretched caressingly?
'Ah, fondest, blindest, weakest,
I am He Whom thou seekest!
Thou dravest love from thee, who dravest Me.'

John Wilhelm Rowntree
1868–1905

Rowntree has just been told by the doctor that he will become totally blind.

Dazed and overwhelmed he staggered from the doctor's office to the street and stood there in silence. Suddenly he felt the love of God wrap him about as though a visible presence enfolded him, and a joy filled him such as he had never known before. From that time he was a gloriously joyous and happy man.

Man's Relation to God

Henry Handel Richardson
1870–1946

For the book open before Richard, in which he was making notes as he read, was the Bible. Bending over him to drop a kiss on top of his head, Polly had been staggered by what she saw. Opposite the third verse of the first chapter of Genesis: 'And God said, Let there be light; and there was light', he had written 'Three days before the sun!' Her heart seemed to shrivel, to grow small in her breast, at the thought of her husband being guilty of such an impiety. Standing there under the stars, she said aloud, as if someone, the One, could hear her: 'He doesn't mean to do wrong, I know he doesn't!' But when she re-entered the room, he was still at it. His beautiful handwriting, reduced to its tiniest, wound round the narrow margins.

The Fortunes of Richard Mahoney

9

From Miguel Unamuno to Carolyn M. Rodgers:
20th–21st century

Miguel Unamuno
1864–1936

For me, God is not a rational necessity; I have no need of Him to explain the universe: what I cannot explain without God I cannot explain with Him. But he can become a need of the heart, the revelation of the Father. I realise that all this will strike you as a kind of jumble, like everything that happens when one attempts to reason with one's heart, which is as bad as trying to feel with one's head (in the everyday sense).

Inasmuch as I don't expect God to explain anything, I do not make a dogma of my own out of Him, nor even an ideal. God is continuously evolving in me, in my consciousness. Does this correspond with outer reality? I don't know.

Selected Works of Miguel Unamuno

W. B. Yeats
1865–1939

One day I was walking over a bit of marshy ground close to Inchy Wood when I felt, all of a sudden, and only for a second, an emotion which I said to myself was the root of a Christian mysticism. There had swept over me a sense of weakness, of dependence on a great personal Being somewhere far off yet near at hand. No thought of mine had prepared me for this emotion, for I had been preoccupied with Aengus and Edain, and with Manannan, Son of the Sea. That night I awoke lying upon my back and hearing a voice speaking above me and saying: 'No human soul is like any other human soul, and therefore the love of God for any human soul is infinite, for no other soul can satisfy the same need in God.'

Mythologies

Rainer Maria Rilke
1875–1926

The Olive Garden

And still he climbed, and through the grey leaves thrust,
quite grey and lost in the grey olive lands,
and laid his burning forehead full of dust
deep in the dustiness of burning hands.

After all, this. And this, then, was the end.
Now I'm to go, while I am going blind,
and, oh, why wilt Thou have me still contend
Thou art, whom I myself no longer find.

No more I find Thee. In myself no tone
of Thee; nor in the rest; nor in this stone.
I can find Thee no more. I am alone.

I am alone with all that human fate
I undertook through Thee to mitigate,
Thou who art not. Oh, shame too consummate . . .

An angel came, those afterwards relate.

Wherefore an angel? Oh, there came the night,
and turned the leaves of trees indifferently,
and the disciples stirred uneasily.
Wherefore an angel? Oh, there came the night.

The night that came requires no specifying;
just so a hundred nights go by,
while dogs are sleeping and while stones are lying –
just any melancholy night that, sighing,
lingers till morning mount the sky.

For angels never come to such men's prayers,
nor nights for them mix glory with their gloom.
Forsakenness is the self-loser's doom,
and such are absent from their father's cares
and disincluded from their mother's womb.

Evelyn Underhill
1875–1941

Letter to M.R. 1909

I think it helps one to go on if one remembers that one's
true relation to God is not altered by the fact that one has
ceased to be aware of it. Other things being equal, you are
just where you were before, but are temporarily unable to
see the Light. And the use of the disability, just like the use
of any other sort of suffering, is to prevent you from
identifying fullness of life with fullness of comfort. Your
ideal of spiritual life must be right up above all the
pleasure-and-pain oscillations of your finite, restless self:

and you will not have any real peace till you have surrendered that self altogether, and tried to grasp nothing, not even love. When you absolutely and eagerly surrender yourself to the Will, you will cease to write under that sense of deprivation. You will take all in the day's work and go on steadily. These are the sort of times when verbal prayer, if one has assimilated it and made it one's own in more genial seasons, becomes a help: and enables one to go doggedly on, praying more, not less, because the light is withdrawn. To do otherwise would be a confession that you have been living by sight and not really by faith at all ... The true attitude is to rest with entire trustfulness on the Love of God, and not care two straws what happens to one's self. If you are there how little the question of whether you see you are there can matter. It is rather an honour to be allowed to serve him in the darkness instead of being given a night-light like a nervous child.

Andrew Young
1885–1971

Nicodemus

O risen Lord,
I do not ask you to forgive me now;
There is no need.
I came to-night to speak to your dead body,
To touch it with my hands and say 'Forgive,'
For though I knew it could not speak to me
Or even hear, yet it was once yourself;
It is dissolved and risen like a dew,
And now I know,
As dawn forgives the night, as spring the winter,

You have forgiven me. It is enough.
Why do I kneel before your empty tomb?
You are not here, for you are everywhere;
The grass, the trees, the air, the wind, the sky,
Nothing can now refuse to be your home;
Nor I. Lord, live in me and I shall live.
This is the word you spoke,
The whole earth hears it, for the whole earth cries,
I AM THE RESURRECTION, AND THE LIFE: HE THAT
BELIEVETH IN ME THOUGH HE WERE DEAD, YET
SHALL HE LIVE: AND WHOSOEVER LIVETH AND
BELIEVETH IN ME SHALL NEVER DIE.

Edwin Muir
1887–1959

Last night, going to bed alone, I suddenly found myself (I was taking off my waistcoat) reciting the Lord's Prayer in a loud emphatic voice – a thing I had not done for many years – with deep urgency and profound disturbed emotion.

While I went on I grew more composed; as if it had been empty and craving and were being replenished, my soul grew still; every word had a strange fullness of meaning which astonished and delighted me. It was late; I had sat up reading; I was sleepy; but as I stood in the middle of the floor half-undressed, saying the prayer over and over, meaning after meaning sprang from it, overcoming me again with joyful surprise; and I realised that this simple repetition was always universal and always inexhaustible, and day by day sanctified human life.

An Autobiography

Katherine Butler Hathaway
1890–1942

Then one day I found somewhere, on a page I have since forgotten, three words which had greater power than even the doctor's words. When I began to feel the horror coming on, I said to myself, 'God within me ... God within me ... God within me ...' While I was saying those three words I felt and I knew that I was no longer alone. All of a sudden, because of those three words, I could walk along the street without fear. Saying 'God within me' brought me an inrush of quietness and sweetness, a feeling inside me of dignity and wholeness which was not me at all, but something greater than I was, against which the horrors were powerless. Just by saying, over and over and believing as I said it, 'God within me, God within me,' I could send entirely out of myself the quick-spreading toxic fear and the disintegration it created. Perhaps this was a symbolic experience by which I unconsciously found relief for my sexual starvation. Perhaps the miraculous sense of peace which I got from saying 'God within me' was a trick of the unconscious which substituted a religious ecstasy for an ecstasy of the body. If this is true it only means that both ecstasies have the same source, they are friends and they are both divine.

The Little Locksmith

Dorothy Day
1897–1980

'All my life I have been haunted by God', a character in one of Dostoevsky's books says. And that is the way it was with me.

It began out in California, where the family had moved from New York a year before. We were living in Berkeley in a furnished house, waiting for our furniture to come around the Horn. It was Sunday afternoon in the attic. I remember the day was very chilly, though there were roses and violets and calla lilies blooming in the garden. My sister and I had been making dolls of the calla lilies, putting rosebuds for heads at the top of the long graceful blossoms. Then we made perfume, crushing flowers into a bottle with a little water in it. Even now I can remember the peculiar delicious, pungent smell.

And then I remember we were in the attic. I was sitting behind a table, pretending I was the teacher, reading aloud from a Bible that I had found. Slowly, as I read, a new personality impressed itself on me. I was being introduced to someone and I knew almost immediately that I was discovering God.

From Union Square to Rome

C. S. Lewis
1898–1963

I was going up Headington Hill [Oxford] on the top of a bus. Without words and (I think) almost without images, a fact about myself was somehow presented to me. I became aware that I was holding something at bay, or shutting something out. Or, if you like, that I was wearing some stiff clothing, like corslets, or even a suit of armour, as if I were a lobster. I felt myself being, there and then, given a free choice. I could open the door or keep it shut; I could unbuckle the armour or keep it on. Neither choice was presented as a duty; no threat or promise was attached to either, though I knew that to open the door or to take off the corslet meant the incalculable. The choice appeared to be momentous but it was also strangely unemotional. I was moved by no desires or fears. In a sense I was not moved by anything. I chose to open, to unbuckle, to loosen the rein. I say, 'I chose,' yet it did not really seem possible to do the opposite. On the other hand, I was aware of no motives. You could argue that I was not a free agent, but I am more inclined to think that this came nearer to being a perfectly free act than most that I have ever done. Necessity may not be the opposite of freedom, and perhaps a man is most free when, instead of producing motives, he could only say, 'I am what I do.' Then came the repercussion on the imaginative level. I felt as if I were a man of snow at long last beginning to melt. The melting was starting in my back – drip-drip and presently trickle-trickle. I rather disliked the feeling.

Surprised by Joy

Antonia White
1899–1979

1940
All I know is that an eye seemed to open somewhere inside me, an eye very filmed and feeble, seeing nothing definite but yet knowing that there was something to see.

Diary

Jorge Luis Borges
1899–1986

Diodorus Siculus tells the story of a god, broken and scattered abroad. What man of us has never felt, walking through the twilight or writing down a date from his past, that he has lost something infinite?

Mankind has lost a face, an irretrievable face, and all have longed to be that pilgrim – imagined in the Empyrean, beneath the Rose – who in Rome sees the Veronica and murmurs in faith, 'Lord Jesus, my God, true God, is this then what Thy face was like?'

Beside a road there is a stone face and an inscription that says, 'The True Portrait of the holy Face of the God of Jaén.' If we truly knew what it was like, the key to the parables would be ours and we would know whether the son of the carpenter was also the Son of God.

Paul saw it as a light that struck him to the ground; John, as the sun when it shines in all its strength; Teresa de Jesús saw it many times, bathed in tranquil light, yet she was never sure of the color of His eyes.

We lost those features, as one may lose a magic number made up of the usual ciphers, as one loses an image in a kaleidoscope, forever. We may see them and know them not. The profile of a Jew in the subway is perhaps the profile of Christ; perhaps the hands that give us our change at a ticket window duplicate the ones some soldiers nailed one day to the cross.

Perhaps a feature of the crucified face lurks in every mirror; perhaps the face died, was erased, so that God may be all of us.

Who knows but that tonight we may see it in the labyrinth of dreams, and tomorrow not know we saw it.

Dreamtigers

Graham Greene
1904–1991

My friend Antonia White many years later told me how, while she was attending the funeral of her father, an old priest, who had known her as a child, tried to persuade her to return to the Church. At last – to please him more than for any other reason – she said, 'Well then father, remind me of the reasons for the existence of God'. After a long hesitation, he admitted to her, 'I knew them once but I have forgotten them'. I have suffered the same loss of memory. I can only remember that in January 1926, I became convinced of the probable existence of something we call God.

A Sort of Life

Simone Weil

1909–1943

There is only one time when I really know nothing of this certitude [of belief in God] any longer. It is when I am in contact with the affliction of other people, those who are indifferent or unknown to me as much as the others, perhaps even more, including those of the most remote ages of antiquity. This contact causes me such atrocious pain and so utterly rends my soul, that as a result the love of God becomes almost impossible for me for a while. It would take very little more to make me say impossible. So much so that I am uneasy about myself, I reassure myself a little by remembering that Christ wept on foreseeing the horrors of the destruction of Jerusalem. I hope he will forgive me my compassion.

Waiting on God

Albert Camus

1913–1960

Tarrou asks Dr Rieux, exhausted from treating plague victims, why he shows so much devotion when he doesn't believe in God.

'I've never managed to get used to seeing people die. That's all I know. Yet after all . . .'

Rieux fell silent, and sat down. He felt his mouth dry.

'After all . . . ?' Tarrou prompted softly.

'After all,' the doctor repeated, then hesitated again, fixing his eyes on Tarrou, 'it's something that a man of your sort can understand most likely, but, since the order of the world is shaped by death, mightn't it be better for God if we refuse to believe in Him, and struggle with all our might against death, without raising our eyes towards the heaven where He sits in silence?'

Tarrou nodded.

'Yes. But your victories will never be lasting; that's all.'

'Yes. I know that. But it's no reason for giving up the struggle.'

'No reason, I agree . . . Only, I now can picture what this plague must mean for you.'

'Yes. A never-ending defeat.'

The Plague

Thomas Merton
1915–1968

A door opens in the center of our being and we seem to fall through it into immense depths which, although they are infinite, are all accessible to us; all eternity seems to have become ours in this one placid and breathless contact.

God touches us with a touch that is emptiness, and empties us. He moves us with a simplicity that simplifies us. All variety, all complexity, all paradox, all multiplicity cease. Our mind swims in the air of an understanding, a reality that is dark and serene and includes in itself everything. Nothing more is desired. Nothing more is wanting. Our only sorrow, if sorrow be possible at all, is the awareness that we ourselves still live outside of God.

The Seeds of Contemplation

Love sails me around the house. I walk two steps on the

ground and four steps in the air. It is love. It is consolation. I don't care if it is consolation. I am not attached to consolation. I love God. Love carries me all around. I don't want to *do* anything but love.

And when the bell rings, it is like pulling teeth to make myself shift because of that love, hidden love, obscure love, down inside me and outside me, where I don't care to talk about it. Anyway, I don't have the time or the energy to discuss such matters. I have only time for eternity, which is to say, for love, love, love.

Maybe Saint Teresa would like to have me snap out of it, but it is pure, I tell you: I am not attached to it (I hope) and it is love, and it gives me soft punches all the time in the center of my heart. Love is pushing me around the monastery, love is kicking me all around, like a gong, I tell you. Love is the only thing that makes it possible for me to continue to tick.

The Sign of Jonas

January 27, 1950
Today, in a moment of trial, I rediscovered Jesus, or perhaps discovered Him for the first time. But then, in a monastery you are always discovering Jesus for the first time. Anyway, I came closer than ever to fully realising how true it is that our relations with Jesus are something utterly beyond the level of imagination and emotion.

His eyes, which are the eyes of Truth, are fixed upon my heart. Where His glance falls, there is peace: for the light of His Face, which is the Truth, produces truth wherever it shines. His eyes are always on us in choir and everywhere and in all times. No grace comes to us from heaven except He looks upon our hearts.

The grace of this gaze of Christ upon my heart transfigured this day like a miracle. It seems to me that I have discovered a freedom that I never knew before in my life and with this freedom a recollection that is no impediment to moderate action. I have felt the Spirit of God upon me, and after dinner, walking along the road beyond the orchard by myself under a cobalt blue sky (in which the moon was already visible) I thought that, if I only turned my head a little, I would see a tremendous host of angels in silver armour advancing behind me through the sky, coming at last to sweep the whole world clean. I did not have to mortify this fantasy as it did not arouse my emotions but carried me along on a vivid ocean of peace. And the whole world and the whole sky were filled with a wonderful music, as it has often been for me in these days. Sitting alone in the attic of the garden house and looking at the stream shining under the bare willows and at the distant hills, I think I have never been so near to Adam's, my father's, Eden. Our Eden is the heart of Christ.

Entering the Silence: Journals

Philip Toynbee
1916–1981

21st August
We played Haydn's Nelson Mass yesterday evening, and this was one of those rare occasions of great exaltation. But even then I felt that almost painful yearning; the sense of a vast promise not quite fulfilled. As if the rising line of the graph always reaches the end of the paper some distance from the top. And so I extrapolate from that high point of Earthly beauty, and imagine a continuation of the line in Heaven.

But I suppose the supreme secular experience is falling in love. The Beloved is praised by the Lover in terms which seem wildly extravagant, even deluded, to a friend. But perhaps this is because the Lover has seen God in the loved face: has drawn God down into the loved face, body, temperament, mind: soul.

Part of a Journey 1977–1979

George Mackay Brown
1921–1996

Yet no Scotsman takes precipitate action. I lingered for years in this state of acknowledging Catholicism, while doing nothing about it. In the Scottish town of Dalkeith near where I was studying in 1951/2, I went to mass twice or thrice and was disappointed – I got lost in the Missal, among the long silences and the whispers; and the hymns and the worshippers with their beads were strange to me. The devotion of the working-class women did move me: here they found beauty and peace in the midst of drab lives.

Yet I felt that, in spite of all, here was the Church that had been founded on the Rock.

And still I delayed, for another ten years.

In the end it was literature that broke down my last defences. There are many ways of entering a fold; it was the beauty of words that opened the door to me:

Love bade me welcome; yet my soul drew back, guilty of dust and sin . . .

The beauty of Christ's parables was irresistible. How could they fail to be, when so many of them concern ploughing and seedtime and harvest, and his listeners were most of them fishermen? I live in a group of islands that have been farmed for many centuries; all round me in summer are the whispering cornfields turning from green to gold. 'Except a seed fall into the ground, and die . . .' Those words were a delight and a revelation, when I first understood them. And at piers and moorings in every village and island are the fishing boats, and the daily venturers into the perilous west, the horizon-eyed, salt-tongued fishermen ('The kingdom is like a net . . .'; 'I will make you fishers of men . . .'). The elements of earth and sea, that we thought so dull and ordinary, held a bounteousness and a mystery not of this world. Now I looked with another eye at those providers of our bread and fish; and when I came at last to work as a writer, it was those heroic and primeval occupations that provided the richest imagery, the most exciting symbolism.

That the toil of the earthworker should become in the Mass, Corpus Christi, was a wonder beyond words, and still is. That one of the Pope's titles is The Fisherman, an acknowledgement of his descent from Simon Peter the fisherman, was an added delight to the mind and spirit, and still is.

'You must sit down' says Love, 'and taste my meat.'
So I did sit and eat.

For the Islands I Sing: An Autobiography

Michael Hollings
1921–1997

When a person is set down before God, is trying hard to be recollected, is even trying to think of God and Christ, and all that happens is that there is a blank, an emptiness, a pain, it is not easy to get across to that person that all is well and this is as it should be! BUT IT IS AS IT SHOULD BE!

Day by Day

Brian Moore

1921–

An ancient monastery on an Irish island refuses to change its liturgy after 'Vatican III' and the Abbot finds himself challenging Rome and an emissary sent to confront him.

The Abbot sighed. Years ago, he would have knelt and offered up an act of contrition for his unruly temper. But, years ago, he had felt a certainty about so many things. Aggiornamento, was that when uncertainty had begun? Changes of Doctrine. Setting oneself up as ultimate authority. Insubordination. He looked at the tabernacle. Insubordination. The beginning of breakdown. And, long ago, that righteous prig at Wittenberg nailing his defiance to the church door.

The Abbot rose. He did not genuflect. He went down the side aisle and out into the night.

Catholics

Shusaku Endo

1923–1996

The 'martyrs' in this short story are Japanese villagers who are tortured for being Christians. One of them, Kisuke, is considered a Judas for recanting his faith. While the surviving villagers await further torture and death in prison, they are amazed to see Kisuke, who found courage while sitting on a beach.

Listening to the sound of the dark waves that pushed in and broke, broke and then retreated, Kisuke felt a bitterness towards God surging up from the depths of his heart. There are two types of people – those born with strong hearts and courage, and those who are craven and clumsy. But me – I'm spineless by nature, and my knees buckle and I turn pale if someone just lifts a hand against me. Because I was born like that, even though I want to believe in the Lord Jesus' teachings, in no way can I put up with torture.

If only I hadn't been born in these times.

If Kisuke had lived in the distant past when freedom of religion was accessible, even if he had not been one of the valiant souls, he wouldn't have ended up in this predicament of betraying the Lord Jesus and Santa Maria.

Why was I born to such a fate?

That thought made Kisuke resent God's lack of compassion.

It happened just as Kisuke stood and was about to leave the beach. He heard a voice calling to him from behind. He turned round, but no one was there. It was neither the voice of a man nor a woman. But he had heard the voice echoing clearly amidst the sound of the black ocean waves.

'All you have to do is go and be with the others. If you're tortured again and you become afraid, it's all right to run away. It's all right to betray me. But go follow the others.'

Kisuke stopped in his tracks and looked out at the sea in a daze. He pressed his fists against his face and wept aloud.

When Kisuke had finished his story, the Christians in the cell were silent, emitting not even a cough. As they sat in confinement they knew from the sharp stab at their skin that the snow was gradually piling up outside. Kanzaburo felt that the tortures he had endured these two years, and the fact that his brother had died without abandoning the faith, had not been in vain.

The next morning the officers unlocked the door to the one-metre cell to interrogate Kisuke. If Kisuke would not agree to apostatize, he would be thrown into the icy lake in the garden of the temple. As he listened to the rasp of the lock and to Kisuke's faltering footsteps, Kanzaburo whispered: 'Kisuke. If it hurts you, it's all right to apostasize. It's all

right. The Lord Jesus is pleased just because you came here.
He is pleased.'

The Final Martyrs

Zbigniew Herbert
1924–1998

Voice

I walk on the sea-shore
to catch that voice
between the breaking of one wave
and another

but there is no voice
only the senile garrulity of water
salty nothing
a white bird's wing
stuck dry to a stone

I walk to the forest
where persists the continuous
hum of an immense hour-glass
sifting leaves into humus
humus into leaves
powerful jaws of insects
consume the silence of the earth

I walk into the fields
green and yellow sheets
fastened with pins of insects beings
sing at every touch of the wind

where is that voice
it should speak up
when for a moment there is a pause
in the unrelenting monologue of the earth

nothing but whispers
clappings explosions

I come home
and my experience takes on
the shape of an alternative
either the world is dumb
or I am deaf
but perhaps we are both
doomed to our afflictions

therefore we must
arm in arm
go blindly on
towards new horizons
towards contracted throats
from which rises
an unintelligible gurgle.

Elizabeth Jennings

1926–2001

Among the Stars

I walked into our garden one spring night,
    Warmth moved among the trees,
The stars were plentiful and in their light
I felt an exaltation such as is

Offered at times but never earned. I was
　　　Caught by a wonder which
I'd never heard of. Now it is a grace,
That night the very Heavens seemed to reach

Down to my stance. My spirit and my flesh
　　　Were one existence then.
How often since has such joy been my wish
As then was granted to a child of ten.

Martin Luther King
1929–1968

It was not until I became a part of the leadership of the Montgomery bus protest that I was actually confronted with the trials of life. Almost immediately after the protest had been undertaken, we began to receive threatening telephone calls and letters in our home. Sporadic in the beginning, they increased day after day. At first I took them in my stride, feeling that they were the work of a few hotheads who would become discouraged after they discovered that we would not fight back. But as the weeks passed, I realized that many of the threats were in earnest. I felt myself faltering and growing in fear.

After a particularly strenuous day, I settled in bed at a late hour. My wife had already fallen asleep and I was about to doze off when the telephone rang. An angry voice said, 'Listen, Nigger, we've taken all we want from you. Before next week you'll be sorry you ever came to Montgomery.' I hung up, but I could not sleep. It seemed that all of my fears had come down on me at once. I had reached the saturation point.

I got out of bed and began to walk the floor. Finally, I went to the kitchen and heated a pot of coffee. I was ready to give up. I tried to think of a way to move out of the picture without appearing to be a coward. In this state of exhaustion, when my courage had almost gone, I determined to take my problem to God. My head in my hands, I bowed over the kitchen table and prayed aloud. The words I spoke to God that midnight are still vivid in my memory. 'I am here taking a stand for what I believe is right. But now I am afraid. The people are looking to me for leadership, and if I stand before them without strength and courage, they too will falter. I am at the end of my powers. I have nothing left. I've come to the point where I can't face it alone.'

At that moment I experienced the presence of the Divine as I had never before experienced him. It seemed as though I could hear the quiet assurance of an inner voice, saying, 'Stand up for righteousness, stand up for truth. God will be at your side forever.' Almost at once my fears began to pass from me. My uncertainty disappeared. I was ready to face anything. The outer situation remained the same, but God had given me inner calm.

Three nights later, our home was bombed. Strangely enough, I accepted the word of the bombing calmly. My experience with God had given me a new strength and trust. I knew now that God is able to give us the interior resources to face the storms and problems of life.

Let this affirmation be our ringing cry. It will give us courage to face the uncertainties of the future. It will give our tired feet new strength as we continue our forward stride toward the city of freedom. When our days become dreary with low-hovering clouds and our nights become darker than a thousand midnights, let us remember that there is a great benign Power in the universe whose name is God, and he is able to make a way out of no way, and transform dark yesterdays into bright tomorrows. This is our hope for becoming better men. This is our mandate for seeking to make a better world.

Strength to Love

Margaret Fishback Powers

Footprints

One night a man had a dream. He dreamt he was walking along the beach with his Lord. Across the sky flashed scenes from his life.

For each scene he noticed two sets of footprints in the sand, one belonging to him, the other to the Lord. When the last scene in his life flashed before him he looked back at the footprints on the sand. He noticed that many times along the path of his life there was only one set of footprints. He also noticed that it happened at the very lowest and saddest times of his life.

This really bothered him, and he questioned the Lord about it. 'Lord, you said that, once I decided to follow you, you would walk with me all the way. But I've noticed that during the most difficult times in my life there is only one set of footprints. I don't understand why, in times when I needed you most, you would leave me.'

The Lord replied, 'My precious child, I love you and would never leave you during your trials and sufferings; when you see only one set of footprints, it was then that I carried you.'

Geoffrey Hill

1932–

Lachrimae Amantis

What is there in my heart that you should sue
so fiercely for its love? What kind of care

brings you as though a stranger to my door
through the long night and in the icy dew

seeking the heart that will not harbour you,
that keeps itself religiously secure?

At this dark solstice filled with frost and fire
your passion's ancient wounds must bleed anew.

So many nights the angel of my house
has fed such urgent comfort through a dream,
whispered, 'your lord is coming, he is close'

that I have drowsed half-faithful for a time
bathed in pure tones of promise and remorse:
'tomorrow I shall wake to welcome him.'

Imants Ziedonis

1933−

The Mystery

We uncovered a mystery. We slowly drew back the veil from
its face − there it lay, an unspecified form, overdue and precipitate, clearly beyond comprehension, with something
concealed in its core, and we felt quite certain that this was
a mystery and, as such, it had to be probed and uncovered;
with great care we drew back its veil, and now it appeared
before us, a genuine mystery − not paid for, nor ever
encountered − and gleamed like firewood which soon was
to burn, and we certainly wanted an insight and wanted to
know; we drew back its coverings, and uncovered the
mystery: crosswise, it lay like a breeze that was lost, and there
was no knowing if it was weighty or merely pretended to be

so; or if it indeed was a mystery; if it was, though, we had to uncover it; eager, all eyes, we uncovered the mystery: it now was at last a genuine and more than genuine mystery, alarmingly small and becoming still smaller and smaller, and seemingly farther and farther away, and we feared we might lose the mystery, and no longer wished to uncover it.

We were left with strange veils in our hands. Like proof of our wish to uncover something or other.

Epiphanies

Vaclav Havel
1936–

June 19, 1982

Dear Olga,
Again, I call to mind that distant moment in Hermanice when on a hot, cloudless summer day, I sat on a pile of rusty iron and gazed into the crown of an enormous tree that stretched, with dignified repose, up and over all the fences, wires, bars and watchtowers that separated me from it. As I watched the imperceptible trembling of its leaves against an endless sky, I was overcome by a sensation that is difficult to describe: all at once, I seemed to rise above all the co-ordinates of my momentary existence in the world into a kind of state outside time in which all the beautiful things I had ever seen and experienced existed in a total 'co-present'; I felt a sense of reconciliation, indeed of an almost gentle consent to the inevitable course of things as revealed to me now, and this combined with a carefree determination to face what had to be faced. A profound amazement at the sovereignty of Being became a dizzying sensation of tumbling endlessly into the abyss of its mystery; an unbounded joy at being alive, at having been given the

chance to live through all I have lived through, and at the fact that everything has a deep and obvious meaning – this joy formed a strange alliance in me with a vague horror at the inapprehensibility and unattainability of everything I was so close to in that moment, standing at the very 'edge of the finite'; I was flooded with a sense of ultimate happiness and harmony with the world and myself, with that moment, with all the moments I could call up, and with everything invisible that lies behind it and which has meaning. I would even say that I was somehow 'struck by love,' though I don't know precisely for whom or what.

Letters to Olga

Jill Paton Walsh
1937–

Beneditx, the medieval monk, has failed to convince the princely atheist Palinor that God exists, and instead has become convinced by Palinor that there is no God.

Beneditx left the pages unturned, set down his quill, and gazed out of his high window. The vale of the Galilea in all its beauty spread out before him, and he could watch the day move across it in a changing panorama of light and shade from dawn to dusk. Once he had seen the world drawn very fine and thin, transfused with the presence of God, a bright immanence giving all things solidity and meaning. God did not merely exist but was present in every atom of his creation, so that every sight and sound was a sacrament, the flight of the smallest bird was a blessing. Now the world had come to seem a brutal and purposeless chaos, wholly contingent, not a noble building but a tumble of stones.

Knowledge of Angels

Carolyn M. Rodgers
1945–

how I got ovah II/It Is Deep II
for Evangelist Richard D. Henton

just when i thought i had gotten away
my mother
called me on the phone
and did not ask,
but commanded me
to come to church with her.

and because i knew so much
and had 'escaped'
i thought it a harmless enough act.

i was not prepared for the Holy Ghost.
i was not prepared to be covered by the
blood of Jesus

i was not ready to be dipped in
                                        the water . . .

i could not drink the water turned wine.

and so i went back another day
trying to understand the mysteries
of mystical life the 'intellectual'
purity of mystical light.
and that Sunday evening while i was
sitting there and the holy gospel choir
was singing
          'oh oh oh oh somebody touched me'

somebody touched me.
                    and when i turned around to
see what it was whoever touched me wanted
my mother leaned over and whispered in my ear
        'musta been the hand of the Lord'

Biographies and Notes

Chapter 2: *From St Matthew to St Hesychios the Priest*
ST ANATOLIUS OF CONSTANTINOPLE d. 458
Patriarch of Constantinople, put to death by heretics.

ST AUGUSTINE 354–430
Born in North Africa, Augustine was 32 when he was converted fully
to Christianity. He became Bishop of Hippo, which then became the
centre of the intellectual life of Western Christianity. His influence
on Christian theology is immense.

JOHN CASSIAN c.360–c.435
Monk and ascetic writer from Southern Gaul and the first to intro-
duce the rules of Eastern monasticism to the West. He founded two
monasteries in Marseilles.

THE GOSPEL OF EVE
The Gnostic *Gospel of Eve* is known only from one or two short quo-
tations from the great heretic-hunter Epiphanius (310/20–402),
Bishop of Salamis.

ST HESYCHIOS THE PRIEST 8th or 9th century
Abbot of the Monastery of the Mother of God of the Burning Bush
(Vatos) in Sinai.

ST IGNATIUS OF ANTIOCH d. 107
A disciple of St John the Evangelist, Ignatius is said to have been
appointed by St Peter as Bishop of Antioch. He was martyred by
being thrown to lions in the Colosseum.

ISAAC OF NINEVEH 7th century
Also known as Isaac of Syria, he was born in the region of Qatar in
the Persian Gulf and ordained Bishop of Nineveh. After five months

he resigned and went to live in solitude in the desert, where he made a study of mysticism.

ST JOHN OF KARPATHOS 7th(?) century
Probably came from the island of Karpathos where he is thought to have been bishop. His writings were primarily aimed at offering encouragement to those tempted to abandon the monastic life.

ST MAKARIOS OF EGYPT 4th century
Coptic monk and desert father, thought to have written the Homilies which are considered to be an expression of Eastern Christian spirituality at its best.

ST MARY OF EGYPT 3rd century
According to legend, she was a former courtesan who lived as a hermitess for 47 years. She later became a popular medieval saint.

ST MAXIMOS THE CONFESSOR 580–662
A Byzantine monk, theologian and ascetical writer who died in exile in the Caucasus after opposing certain heresies.

PAUL THE SIMPLE d. 339
A farmer in Egypt, he became a hermit and disciple of St Anthony at the age of 60.

THE PHILOKALIA
The bible of Orthodox spirituality, it is a collection of mystical and ascetic writings written between the fourth century and the fifteenth.

ABBA SILVANUS d. c.414
A Palestinian who headed a community with 12 disciples.

Chapter 3: *From Bede to St Symeon*
BEDE 673–735
Anglo-Saxon monk, historian and scholar known as the Venerable Bede. He spent his entire life in Northumbria where, in 731 in the monastery at Jarrow, he wrote *Historia Ecclesiastica Gentis Anglorum*.

CAEDMON 7th(?) century
Said by Bede to have been a herdsman and the first English poet, he entered the monastery of Whitby as an old man.

CYNEWULF 8th or 9th century
A Northumbrian or Mercian poet.

ST SYMEON 949–1022
Monk and mystic of the Eastern Church and founder of a monastery near Constantinople. He was frequently persecuted for his ideas and for the strictness of his teaching.

Chapter 4: *From St Anselm to Thomas à Kempis*
ST AELRED OF RIEVAULX 1110–1167
Abbot of the Cistercian monastery at Rievaulx in Yorkshire. He was hailed as the 'Bernard of the North' (after St Bernard of Clairvaux) and wrote his greatest work, *Speculum Caritatis (Mirror of Charity)*, at the request of St Bernard.

ANGELA OF FOLIGNO 1248–1309
After the death of her husband and children she practised complete Franciscan poverty. Her visions were written down by her uncle, a Franciscan friar.

ST ANSELM 1033–1109
Monk and abbot at the famous Norman monastery of Bec, and later Archbishop of Canterbury; he is best remembered for his philosophical and theological works.

BERNARD OF CLAIRVAUX 1091–1153
The most influential figure in twelfth-century Western Christianity. His writings ushered in a golden age of medieval spirituality. Bernard founded the Cistercian monastery at Clairvaux where he was abbot until his death.

THE CLOUD OF UNKNOWING 14th century
Written by a fourteenth-century English mystic, perhaps a cloistered monk, addressed to a young recluse; he was clearly a great contemplative, but also a keen, sometimes irritable, observer of his fellow men.

DANTE ALIGHIERI 1265–1321
Florentine author of one of Western culture's greatest and works, *The Divine Comedy*, a poetic journey through Hell, Purgatory and Heaven.

MEISTER ECKHART 1260–1329
A German Dominican intellectual and preacher whose challenging work was condemned as heretical by the Church in his day but was embraced by all the great Christian mystics.

HADEWIJCH OF ANTWERP 13th century
One of the great Beguine (see Mechthild of Magdeburg) mystical writers, she wrote in Flemish, her mother tongue.

JACOPONE DA TODI *c.*1228/1230–1306
An ambitious lawyer who converted in middle life, he was a follower of Francis of Assisi.

JESU DULCIS MEMORIA late 12th century
This was attributed to Bernard of Clairvaux, but is now thought to be by an Englishman.

JULIAN OF NORWICH *c.*1343–*c.*1420
A Norfolk gentlewoman and anchoress. All her writings are extended meditations on the visions or 'showings' of the Passion, which she received at the age of 30.

MARGERY KEMPE *c.*1373–*c.*1439
Daughter of the mayor of King's Lynn in Norfolk. She received visions during a period of madness and became a fierce denouncer of all worldly pleasures.

RAMÓN LULL *c.*1233–*c.*1315
Lull was a knight in the service of James I of Majorca when he had a vision of Christ. He became a lay missionary, devoting 50 years of his long life to missionary work, especially among the Moors.

MECHTHILD OF MAGDEBURG 1207–1282/97
Had her first vision at the age of 12. In 1235 she joined a community of Beguines (independent groups of lay women dedicated to religious lives), where her visions, with their intense theme of bridal mysticism, were written down.

RULMAN MERSWIN 1310–1382
An Austrian merchant, he was one of the leaders of the Friends of God, an informal brotherhood of Catholics who practised an often extreme asceticism.

QUIA AMORE LANGUEO 14th or 15th century
'I am sick with love' (Canticles 2:5).

RICHARD ROLLE 1300–1349
After going to Oxford, Rolle became a hermit in Hampole in Yorkshire. His mystical experiences were most often expressed in songs.

HENRY SUSO 1300–1365
German mystic, celebrated preacher, and disciple of Eckhart. He was foremost among the Friends of God (see Rulman Merswin).

JOHN TAULER c.1300–1361
A German Dominican, the greatest of the leaders of the Friends of God (see Rulman Merswin).

THOMAS À KEMPIS 1380–1471
Born near Cologne, he became an Augustinian friar, living most of his life in a community near Zwolle, where he wrote *The Imitation of Christ*.

Chapter 5: *From Martin Luther to Ben Jonson*
ST ALONSO (RODRIGUEZ), THE DOORKEEPER late 16th century
Was not accepted as a priest but spent his life as a lay brother and doorkeeper for the Jesuits in Palma de Mallorca.

MYLES COVERDALE 1488–1568
Early reformer and Lutheran. He published the first English Bible, 1535, and became Bishop of Exeter.

ST IGNATIUS LOYOLA 1491–1556
A former soldier, Ignatius studied for eleven years after undergoing a profound religious experience, which was later to influence the Ignatian Exercises. In 1534, he and six others founded a brotherhood, which would, in 1540, become the Society of Jesus.

ST JOHN OF THE CROSS 1542–1591
The poet and founder of the Discalced Carmelites, St John of the Cross was the spiritual companion and confessor of St Teresa of Avila. Imprisoned and later exiled for his reformist views, his works, including *The Spiritual Canticle*, *The Ascent of Mount Carmel* and *The*

Dark Night of the Soul are among the greatest and most important mystical works ever written.

BEN JONSON 1572/3–1637
Poet, dramatist and friend of Shakespeare. He became a Catholic during imprisonment for killing a fellow actor, but later returned to Anglicanism.

LUIS DE LEÓN 1528–1591
A Spanish Augustinian monk and one of Spain's greatest poets.

MARTIN LUTHER 1483–1546
Luther's 95 theses on indulgences, pinned to the door of the church at Wittenberg, Germany, is often considered to have sparked the Reformation.

ST TERESA OF AVILA 1515–1582
One of the greatest of the Spanish mystics and author of *The Interior Castle*, Teresa was born to a noble family and joined the Carmelite convent in Avila at the age of 21. She chronicles her relationship with God and stresses the 'friendship' between God and man that should be the hallmark of prayer. She was a reformer, founding 17 Discalced (or 'barefoot') Carmelite convents.

LOPE FELIX DE VEGA CARPIO 1562–1635
Spanish poet and playwright.

Chapter 6: *From Marina of Escobar to Cotton Mather*
LANCELOT ANDREWES 1555–1626
Andrewes was successively the Bishop of Chichester, of Ely and of Winchester, and was a hugely popular preacher. He was one of the translators of the Authorised Version of the Bible.

ANNE BRADSTREET 1612–1672
Emigrated from England to Massachusetts. It is claimed that Bradstreet is the first poet of the New World.

JOHN BUNYAN 1628–1688
Bunyan spent 12 years in prison for preaching without a licence during which time he wrote his autobiography, *Grace Abounding to the Chief of Sinners* (1666) and began work on *The Pilgrim's Progress*.

JOHN DONNE 1572–1631
Born into a Catholic family, Donne was ordained as a Protestant
cleric in 1615, later becoming Dean of St Paul's. He became one of
the most celebrated preachers of his age and one of its greatest poets –
both secular and religious.

GEORGE FOX 1624–1691
The son of a weaver, he was the founder of the Quakers.

ST FRANCIS DE SALES 1567–1622
A French priest who was said to have converted 40,000 Swiss
Calvinists back to Catholicism. He founded a new religious order.

MATTHEW HALE 1609–1676
A prominent judge and counsel to Archbishop Laud. He was a
prolific poet during the Commonwealth.

GEORGE HERBERT 1593–1633
Member of an aristocratic family, he became a country parson
renowned for his charity and humility. His poems were published
only after his death.

VENERABLE MARINA OF ESCOBAR 1554–1633
A Spanish mystic, she believed she was commanded by God to write
down, or dictate, her revelations.

CHARLES MARSHALL 1637–1698
English Quaker known for his energetic and zealous preaching.

COTTON MATHER 1663–1728
Along with his father Increase, he was one of the major Puritan
voices in New England. Cotton Mather played an important part in
the Salem witch trial persecutions.

BLAISE PASCAL 1623–1662
French mathematician, physicist and philosopher. The 'Amulet' or
'Memorial' was the scrap of parchment that Pascal always wore on
which he had tried to recapture an overwhelming revelation of God.
It was found after his death in the lining of his doublet.

WILLIAM PENN 1644–1718
English Quaker imprisoned four times for his belief, he envisioned a
colony based on religious and political freedoms. He was the founder
of Pennsylvania, where he established freedom of worship.

FRANCIS QUARLES 1592–1644
Poet and writer of devotional works in prose. Having written a gallant defence of Charles I, he fell under Parliamentary displeasure, suffered the loss of his books and manuscripts, and died, it is said, of a broken heart.

ANGELUS SILESIUS (JOHANN SCHEFFLER) 1624–1677
German mystic, court physician, and later a Catholic friar. He published his poems under his pen name, Silesius.

EDWARD TAYLOR c.1644–1729
Poet and divine. He emigrated to Boston in 1668.

JEREMY TAYLOR 1613–1667
Chaplain to Archbishop Laud and Charles I. After being taken prisoner in the Royalist defeat before Cardigan Castle, 1645, he retired to Wales where he wrote most of his works of religious instruction.

THOMAS TRAHERNE c.1634–1674
Son of a Hereford cobbler, he was ordained in 1660. Many of his poems were rediscovered in a notebook picked up on a London bookstall in 1896.

HENRY VAUGHAN 1621–1695
Joined the Royalist forces in the Civil War. After imprisonment, he spent the rest of his life as a physician in Wales. Like George Herbert, with whom he is often compared, Vaughan's poems were published posthumously.

Chapter 7: *From Elizabeth Singer Rowe to William Wordsworth*
WILLIAM BLAKE 1757–1827
As both artist and poet Blake combined a deeply religious vision with a hatred of institutional Christianity and the 'mind-forged manacles' of doctrine.

JAMES BOSWELL 1740–1795
One of the greatest diarists and biographers in the English language. Like his most famous subject Dr Johnson, Boswell also suffered from religious melancholia.

NATHAN COLE 1711–1783
An early American farmer and Separatist who was inspired to write his *Spiritual Travels* after hearing George Whitefield preach.

WILLIAM COWPER 1731–1800
Suffered from acute religious depression movingly described in his auto-
biographical *Memoir*. He found consolation in evangelical Christianity.

JONATHAN EDWARDS 1703–1758
Celebrated preacher who spearheaded New England's religious
revival, The Great Awakening.

JOHANN WOLFGANG VON GOETHE 1749–1832
One of the towering figures in German literature, renowned for his
novels, poetry and dramas, his most famous work was the poetic
drama *Faust*.

HOWELL HARRIS 1714–1773
Lay preacher and one of the founders of Methodism.

SAMUEL JOHNSON 1709–1784
The subject of Boswell's great biography *The Life of Samuel Johnson*.
He is less well known for his troubled religious faith revealed in his
diaries and meditations.

FRIEDRICH GOTTLIEB KLOPSTOCK 1724–1803
Wrote a great religious epic, *Messias,* and created a new emotional
and sometimes ecstatic poetic diction in his poetry.

WILLIAM LAW 1686–1761
Friend of John Wesley. His most celebrated book, *A Serious Call to a
Devout and Holy Life*, had a profound influence on Dr Johnson.

ELIZABETH SINGER ROWE 1674–1737
Under the poetic name Philomela, she was widely praised for her
pious life and verse. Her devotional prose was much reprinted
throughout the eighteenth century.

LAURENCE STERNE 1713–1768
A country pastor and popular preacher; he is most famous for his
innovatory novel *The Life and Opinions of Tristram Shandy*.

THE TREE OF LIFE
Found in the collection *Divine Hymns or Spiritual Songs* belonging to
Joshua Smith of New Hampshire, 1784.

CHARLES WESLEY 1707–1788
Composed many thousands of hymns. Unlike his brother John, he
remained within the Anglican Church.

JOHN WESLEY 1703–1791
One of the founders of Methodism, he brought the Gospel to the neglected poor in the new cities of the industrial revolution.

JOHN WOOLMAN 1720–1772
An American Quaker who was passionately opposed to slavery and sympathetic to the Indians. His journal is one of the classics of spiritual autobiography.

WILLIAM WORDSWORTH 1770–1850
One of the great English Romantic poets who experienced in nature an intense spirituality. *The Excursion* was written in 1799 and published in 1814.

Chapter 8: *From Zilpha Elaw to Henry Handel Richardson*
EMILY BRONTË 1818–1848
The most enigmatic of the three Brontë sisters. Her poetry expresses deeply personal, visionary experiences.

EMILY DICKINSON 1830–1886
Reclusive American poet whose work, often mystical, reflects the intense inner struggle of her later life.

ZILPHA ELAW c.1790–1846
One of the pioneering African-American women preachers. Although a member of a Methodist Episcopal Society, she was never granted a licence to preach. In 1828 she made a daring preaching trip to the slave states and in 1840 crossed the Atlantic to preach in England.

RALPH WALDO EMERSON 1803–1882
Hugely popular American poet. Was ordained as a pastor but resigned because he felt unable to believe in the sacrament of Communion. His work is marked by a mystical reverence for nature.

AUGUSTUS WILLIAM HARE 1792–1834
Much loved vicar of Alton, Hampshire and famous sermoniser.

GERARD MANLEY HOPKINS 1844–1889
Became a Roman Catholic in 1866 and in 1868 joined the Jesuits. His earlier poems expressing a joy in the natural world and sense of religious ecstasy were followed by a period of despair, after 1885,

when Hopkins wrote what are known as the 'Dark Sonnets'.

RICHARD JEFFERIES 1848–1887
English ruralist and visionary. *Story of My Heart* was his spiritual autobiography.

ST JOHN VIANNEY, CURE D'ARS 1786–1869
French parish priest at the remote village of Ars, near Lyons. His
remarkable insights, lightened by common sense, gave him a worldwide
reputation and he was visited by thousands of pilgrims every year.

SØREN KIERKEGAARD 1813–1855
Danish theologian and philosopher, the grandfather of existentialism.

GEORGE MACDONALD 1824–1905
Victorian visionary writer, who was a major influence on the young
C. S. Lewis.

FREDERICK MYERS 1843–1901
Self-styled 'minor poet and an amateur *savant*', at 23 he had a revival-
istic conversion followed by a period of blank agnosticism.

FRIEDRICH NIETZSCHE 1844–1900
German philosopher who rejected Christian morality and pro-
pounded the doctrine of the will to power.

JOHN HENRY NEWMAN 1801–1890
Newman's celebrated conversion to Catholicism at the age of 44 had
a deep influence on nineteenth-century religious life; it was the subject of his autobiography *Apologia Pro Vita Sua*. He was later made a
cardinal by Pope Leo XII.

HENRY HANDEL RICHARDSON 1870–1946
Pen name of Ethel Florence Lindesay Richardson, born in
Melbourne. The three-volume *The Fortunes of Richard Mahoney* is her
most ambitious work but she was also the author of *Maurice Guest*
and, about her schooldays, *The Getting of Wisdom*.

CHRISTINA ROSSETTI 1830–1894
A devout Anglican who expressed her faith through her poems,
which are often pervaded by a sense of melancholy yearning.

JOHN WILHELM ROWNTREE 1868–1905
An English Quaker, he was told in his early twenties that he would

be completely blind and deaf, but in his short life was a successful businessman, minister and author.

JOHN RUSKIN 1819–1900
Best known for his writings on aesthetics, Ruskin was an open critic of the scientific and technological revolutions of the nineteenth century.

ALFRED, LORD TENNYSON 1809–1892
An Anglican, Tennyson's strain of mysticism emerged clearly in later life. *In Memoriam* is a long elegy for his beloved friend A. H. Hallam who died in 1833.

FRANCIS THOMPSON 1859–1907
Years of opium addiction and intense Catholic religious fervour fuelled the dark imagery of Thompson's poetry.

JAMES THOMSON 1834–1882
A former soldier, Thomson's work was characterised by sadness and a sense of loss.

LEO TOLSTOY 1828–1910
After the *Confession* (1879–82) Tolstoy concentrated almost exclusively on the religious life that he believed to be idealised in the peasant. He was excommunicated by the Orthodox Church, arguing that its teachings were not at all consistent with the Gospel.

SOJOURNER TRUTH 1797(?)–1883
Born into slavery and called Isabella, she became an abolitionist, orator, preacher and dictated her autobiography to her neighbour, Olive Gilbert, in 1850.

MRS HUMPHREY (MARY AUGUSTA) WARD 1851–1920
The granddaughter of Thomas Arnold of Rugby. A successful novelist on social and religious themes, *Robert Elsmere* (1888) was her most famous novel.

WALT WHITMAN 1819–1892
Like Wordsworth and Emerson, Whitman's work demonstrates a powerful spiritual attachment to nature.

Chapter 9: *From Miguel Unamuno to Carolyn M. Rodgers*
JORGE LUIS BORGES 1899–1986
Argentinian writer often claimed as the first magical realist. Borges' work is often intensely philosophical and spiritual.

GEORGE MACKAY BROWN 1921–1996
Born and brought up in the Orkneys, Mackay Brown stayed all his life in the islands and converted to Catholicism. His stories and poems are characterised by a deep sense of ancient local history and rural folklore.

ALBERT CAMUS 1913–1960
French novelist, dramatist and essayist born in Algeria. Perhaps most famous for his novels *The Outsider* (1946) and *The Plague* (1948).

DOROTHY DAY 1897–1980
A communist who converted to Catholicism and founded the newspaper *The Catholic Worker*, which was later to become a movement. Day was an outspoken pacifist and always combined left political leanings with a respect for traditional Catholic doctrine.

SHUSAKU ENDO 1923–1996
A Catholic convert at 12, and Japan's greatest Christian writer, Endo's novels and short stories deal almost exclusively with Christian themes.

GRAHAM GREENE 1904–1991
Greene's novels are haunted by strong religious and Catholic themes, particularly of guilt, and moral dilemmas.

KATHERINE BUTLER HATHAWAY 1890–1942
She spent the first fifteen years of her life in bed suffering from a deformed spine, then went on to become a writer. *The Little Locksmith* is Hathaway's moving memoir of her struggle to be released from the bondage of her physical self.

VACLAV HAVEL 1936–
Czech playwright and first post-Soviet president of the Czech Republic. He was a political dissident and human rights activist who spent five years in prison, from where he wrote to his wife Olga.

ZBIGNIEW HERBERT 1924–1998
Polish poet and essayist, he was a member of the Polish Resistance during World War II.

GEOFFREY HILL 1932–
An English poet, born in the West Midlands, whose work is concerned with religious and historical themes.

MICHAEL HOLLINGS 1921–1997
Priest, writer and broadcaster. Hollings was one of the best-known and loved priests in London. At his packed funeral in Westminster Cathedral, 129 of his fellow priests concelebrated.

ELIZABETH JENNINGS 1926–2001
A prize-winning Catholic poet, she spent most of her life in Oxford.

MARTIN LUTHER KING 1929–1968
A symbol of the African-American civil rights struggle and one of the world's most famous non-violent civil rights activists. A Baptist minister with exceptional oratorical skills and personal courage, he received the Nobel Peace Prize in 1964 and was assasssinated in 1968.

CLIVE STAPLES LEWIS 1898–1963
Literary critic, scholar and novelist whose works of Christian apologetics and religious writings have remained popular all over the world.

THOMAS MERTON 1915–68
Trappist monk of Gethsemane Abbey, Kentucky, Merton popularised Christian spirituality for a vast, worldwide readership. His prolific writings include his autobiography, *The Seven-Storey Mountain.*

BRIAN MOORE 1921–
Belfast-born novelist whose books often mine religious ideas. *Catholics* was set at the time of a future 'Third Vatican Council'.

EDWIN MUIR 1887–1959
Born in the Orkney Islands off Scotland, Muir had a vision in which he was witness to Creation. This experience set him on the path to becoming a poet.

RAINER MARIA RILKE 1875–1926
Perhaps the most important German lyric poet of the twentieth century. 'The Olive Garden' is from *New Poems*, in which Rilke dealt with what seemed to him most significant in human civilisation, including incidents in the Old and New Testaments.

MARGARET FISHBACK POWERS
'Footprints', among the most popular spiritual writings in North

America, was written in 1964, and was anonymous until Powers was revealed as its author in 1980. Born in Canada, she has travelled the world as an evangelist with her husband.

CAROLYN M. RODGERS 1945–
Her volume of poetry *how I got ovah: New and Selected Poems* (1975) reveals a change of emphasis from feminist African-American issues to a profound concern with God.

PHILIP TOYNBEE 1916–1981
Novelist, journalist and reviewer.

MIGUEL DE UNAMUNO Y JUGO 1864–1936
Spanish philosopher who was an admirer of Søren Kierkegaard. He was also a dramatist, novelist, poet and short-story writer.

EVELYN UNDERHILL 1875–1941
Influential Anglican writer on the mystics and spiritual life, she became a practising Christian in 1921.

JILL PATON WALSH 1937–
Children's story writer, novelist for adults and author of detective stories. *Knowledge of Angels* was shortlisted for the 1994 Booker Prize.

SIMONE WEIL 1909–43
French Jewish writer, teacher and social activist, Weil was deeply drawn to Catholicism, though she never converted. She died of exhaustion after years of self-imposed austerity, while working in London for the Free French.

ANTONIA WHITE 1899–1979
Novelist who wrote about her unhappy convent childhood in *Frost in May*. She later returned to her faith.

WILLIAM BUTLER YEATS 1865–1939
Born in Sligo an Irish Protestant, Yeats's work reveals his interest in religious themes, though not specifically Christian ones

ANDREW YOUNG 1885–1971
Scottish poet and minister of the Free Church. He was ordained in the Church of England in 1939.

IMANTS ZIEDONIS 1933–
Latvian poet.

Acknowledgements

The editors and publishers would like to thank all those listed below who have granted permission for the use of material in this book. Every effort has been made to trace and identify copyright holders and to secure permission for reproducing material. If any acknowledgements have been omitted, or any rights overlooked, we will be happy to rectify any omissions or make any amendments necessary in future editions.

Chapter 2: *From St Matthew to St Hesychios the Priest*
ST AUGUSTINE
© Henry Chadwick 1991. Reprinted from St Augustine, *Confessions*, translated with an introduction and notes by Henry Chadwick (1991) by permission of Oxford University Press.

Reprinted by permission of the publishers and the Trustees of the Loeb Classical Library from *Augustine: Confessions – Volume II*, Loeb Classical Library, Volume L 27, X vi (8), translated by W. Watts, Cambridge, Mass.: Harvard University Press, 1912. The Loeb Classical Library® is a registered trademark of the President and Fellows of Harvard College.

JOHN CASSIAN
From John Cassian, *Conferences*, translated by E. C. S. Gibson, *Nicene and Post-Nicene Fathers*, 1894, with kind permission of Continuum International Publishing Ltd.

THE GOSPEL OF EVE
From St Epiphanius of Salamis, *Panarion of St Epiphanius, Bishop of Salamis: Selected Passages*, translated and edited by Philip R. Amidon, copyright © 1990 by Philip R. Amidon. Used by permission of Oxford University Press, Inc.

PAUL THE SIMPLE
From Paul the Simple, *The Sayings of the Desert Fathers: The Alphabetical Collection*, translated by Benedicta Ward, SLG, 1975, with kind permission of Continuum International Publishing Ltd.

Chapter 3: **From Bede to St Symeon**
ANON
From 'Christ and Satan', in *Anglo-Saxon Poetry*, translated and edited by S. A. J. Bradley, J. M. Dent, 1984.

ANON
From *The Dream of the Rood*, in *The Anglo-Saxon World: An Anthology*, translated and edited by Kevin Crossley-Holland, Oxford University Press, 1984.

ANON
From *The Phoenix*, lines 70–103, translated by Burton Raffel, in *Poems and Prose from the Old English*, Yale University Press, 1960, 1998.

ANON
From *The Seafarer*, in *The Anglo-Saxon World: An Anthology*, translated and edited by Kevin Crossley-Holland, Oxford University Press, 1984.

CYNEWULF
Elene, from *Advent Lyrics* (part 1 of Cynewulf's Christ in The Exeter Book), lines 1236 ff, in *The Anglo-Saxon World: An Anthology*, translated and edited by Kevin Crossley-Holland, Oxford University Press, 1984.

Chapter 4: **From St Anselm to Thomas à Kempis**
ST ANSELM
From St Anselm, ch. 1, 'Proslogion', in *The Fire and Cloud: An Anthology of Christian Spirituality*, edited by Revd David A. Fleming, 1978, with kind permission of Continuum International Publishing Ltd.

THE CLOUD OF UNKNOWING
From *The Cloud of Unknowing and the Book of Privy Counseling*, chapter iii, edited with an introduction by William Johnston, Doubleday.

From *The Cloud of Unknowing and Other Treaties by an English Mystic of the Fourteenth Century*, ch. 6, p.14, edited by Abbot Justin McCann, 1952, with kind permission of Continuum International Publishing Ltd.

JOHN TAULER
From *Sermon for the Monday before Palm Sunday* in *An Anthology of Mysticism*, edited by Paul de Jaegher, translated by Donald Attwater and others, 1977, with kind permission of Continuum International Publishing Ltd.

Chapter 5: *From Martin Luther to Ben Jonson*
LUIS DE LEÓN
From *The Heavenly Life*, in *Lyrics of Luis de León*, translated by Aubrey F. G. Bell, 1928, with kind permission of Continuum International Publishing Ltd.

ST JOHN OF THE CROSS
St John of the Cross, 'Other verses with a divine meaning', translated by Roy Campbell. Copyright © Roy Campbell, 1951.

From *Dark Night of the Soul*, Book 1, ch. VIII, *The Complete Works of St John of the Cross*, 1934–5, with kind permission of Continuum International Publishing Ltd.

From The Collected Works of St John of the Cross translated by Kieran Kavanaugh, OCD and Otilio Rodriguez, OCD. Copyright © 1964, 1979, 1991 by the Washington Province of Discalced Carmelite Friars, Inc. ICS Publications, 2131 Lincoln Road, N.E. Washington, D.C. 20002-1199 www.icspublications.org.

Chapter 6: *From Marina of Escobar to Cotton Mather*
COTTON MATHER
From *Reserved Memorials*, edited by Worthington C. Ford, in the Massachusetts Historical Society Collections, Series 7, Volume 7.

ANGELUS SILESIUS (JOHANN SCHEFFLER)
From Angelus Silesius (Johann Scheffler), 'The Cherubic Wanderer', 1674, with kind permission of Continuum International Publishing Ltd.

Chapter 7: **From Elizabeth Singer Rowe to William Wordsworth**
GOETHE
Extract from 'Faust's Confession' from Goethe's *Faust*, translated by
Louis MacNeice (Faber & Faber).

Chapter 8: **From Zilpha Elaw to Henry Handel Richardson**
EMILY DICKINSON
Reprinted by permission of the publishers and the Trustees of
Amherst College from *The Poems of Emily Dickinson*, Thomas H.
Johnson, ed., Cambridge, Mass.: The Belknap Press of Harvard
University Press, copyright © 1951, 1955, 1979 by the President and
Fellows of Harvard College.

FREDERICK MYERS
From *The Century Magazine*, quoted in A. N. Wilson, *God's Funeral*,
John Murray, 1999

LEO TOLSTOY
From Leo Tolstoy, *Confession*, translated by David Patterson.
Copyright © 1983 by David Patterson. Used by permission of W. W.
Norton & Company, Inc.

ST JOHN VIANNEY, CURÉ D'ARS
Alfred Monnin, *Life of the Blessed Curé D'Ars*, 1907, with kind
permission of Continuum International Publishing Ltd.

Chapter 9: **From Miguel Unamuno to Carolyn M. Rodgers**
JORGE LUIS BORGES
Reprinted from Jorge Luis Borges, *Dreamtigers*, translated by Mildred
Boyer and Harold Morland. Copyright © 1964, renewed 1992. By
permission of the University of Texas Press.

GEORGE MACKAY BROWN
George Mackay Brown, *For the Islands I Sing*. Copyright © 1977 John
Murray Ltd.

ALBERT CAMUS
From Albert Camus, *The Plague*, Penguin Books and Alfred A. Knopf.

DOROTHY DAY
From *Union Square to Rome*, 1938, quoted in *Dorothy Day: Selected*

Writings, edited by Robert Ellsberg, Maryknoll, NY: Orbis Books, 1992.

GRAHAM GREENE
From Graham Greene, *A Sort of Life*, Random House, Inc.

VACLAV HAVEL
From Vaclav Havel, *Letters to Olga*, translated by Paul Wilson, copyright © 1984 by Rowahlt Taschenbuch Verlag. Translation copyright © 1988 by Paul Wilson. Copyright © 1983 by Vaclav Havel. Used by permission of Alfred A. Knopf, a division of Random House, Inc.

ZBIGNIEW HERBERT
'Voice', from *Zbigniew Herbert: Selected Poems*, pp. 40–41, translated by Czeslaw Milosz and Peter Dale Scott, Penguin Books, 1968. Translation copyright © Czeslaw Milosz and Peter Dale Scott, 1968.

MICHAEL HOLLINGS
From Michael Hollings, *Day by Day*, © McCrimmon Publishing Co Ltd.

BRIAN MOORE
Brian Moore, *Catholics*. Copyright © 1972 Jonathan Cape.

CAROLYN M. RODGERS
'How I got ovah II/It is deep II', from Carolyn M. Rodgers, *How I Got Ovah*, copyright © 1968, 1969, 1970, 1971, 1972, 1973, 1975 by Carolyn M. Rodgers. Used by permission of Doubleday, a division of Random House, Inc.

W. B. YEATS
From W. B. Yeats, *Mythologies*, used by permission of A. P. Watt Ltd on behalf of Michael B. Yeats.

Index